ADVANCE
PRAISE

"I believe leaders of today are facilitators of movements instead of experts on the top of an organization. We need to embrace the unexpected and co-create with people for the unexpected. To use your vulnerability as a vehicle for innovation. To constantly practice instead of organize. I'm thankful that there is finally a book that could inspire us how to practice this."
Lisa Lindström, Chief Executive Officer,
Doberman, awarded Sweden's Best Employer

"Get ready for some deep mind stretching with this great book packed with insights. I've read *Yoga for Leaders* with a big smile and found myself taking pages full of notes. I love books that have a lot of condensed food for thought and starting points for further exploration. It's refreshing that Stefan does not force his view of the future upon the reader. He is a 'possiblist' (his own words) that lets his leaders read in & out, adapt and create their own future. And if that sounds a bit too 'yoga' for you... then you definitely have to read this book!"
Thimon de Jong, Speaker & Founder,
Whetston Strategic Foresight

Published by
LID Publishing Ltd.
One Adam Street, London. WC2N 6LE

31 West 34th Street, 8th Floor, Suite 8004
New York, NY 10001, US

info@lidpublishing.com
www.lidpublishing.com

A member of:

BPR
Business Publishers Roundtable

www.businesspublishersroundtable.com

© Stefan Hyttfors 2016
© LID Publishing Ltd. 2016

Reprinted 2017

Printed in Great Britain by TJ International
ISBN: 978-1-910649-69-5

Cover design: Caroline Li
Page design: Caroline Li & Sara Taheri

YOGA
FOR
LEADERS

HOW TO MANAGE SELF-DISRUPTION IN
A WORLD OF SELF-DESTRUCTION

STEFAN HYTTFORS

LONDON   MONTERREY
MADRID   SHANGHAI
MEXICO CITY BOGOTA
NEW YORK   BUENOS AIRES
BARCELONA SAN FRANCISCO

CONTENTS

Preface   06

Chapter One: Thoughts Are Deadly   10

Chapter Two: The Time Is Always Now   16

Chapter Three: What Arises Will Pass   26

Chapter Four: Breath Is the Bridge   36

Chapter Five: Count Down   42

Chapter Six: Beat Yourself   52

Chapter Seven: Beware the Risk of Ignorance   60

Chapter Eight: It Is (Always) the Best and
Worst of Times   70

Chapter Nine: A Dysfunctional System   78

Chapter Ten: The Idea of Money   90

Chapter Eleven: Power to the People   100

Chapter Twelve: The Power of Networks   107

Chapter Thirteen: No Boss   118

Chapter Fourteen: No School   130

Chapter Fifteen: No Money   144

Chapter Sixteen: No Car   154

Chapter Seventeen: No Oil   164

Chapter Eighteen: No Job   172

Chapter Nineteen: No Country   182

Chapter Twenty: Ask Why   188

Chapter Twenty-One: Support Others   196

Chapter Twenty-Two: The Purpose of Life Is to Live a Purposeful Life   204

Chapter Twenty-Three: Be a Possibilist   210

Chapter Twenty-Four: Good Luck!   216

PREFACE

Yoga teaches us to cure what need not be endured and endure what cannot be cured.

– B.K.S. Iyengar

If you want to learn yoga as in asanas – the stretching exercises on a rubber mat – this is not the book for you. Today, a new generation of leaders is required, and this book is for anyone who wants to be one.

Leader. You decide how to interpret this word. Sometimes you feel lonely and far away from leading anyone or anything. But that is not true. You are not alone – ever. Open your eyes and observe. There is everything but loneliness. Are you in a room without people? Well, observe things instead. What did it take to create the experience you are having right now? Did you do it all by yourself or did someone else make the chair you are sitting in? Are others involved in producing the energy you are consuming right now? Do you smell food, hear music, or sense movement? What, oh you're alone on an airplane … Really?! No pilot today?

Just observe and reflect. There is always so much going on outside and around your physical body. So much, and so many people involved in the making of every moment. You can also do this exercise the other way around. Just imagine this moment as if nothing except you existed. No trees, no buildings, no cars, no animals and no humans. Nothing but you; just a foggy white nothingness.

The illusion of loneliness is a problem that causes self-centered thinking and greed; the root of humanity's greatest challenge. You need to overcome it, since everything you do affects others. Human beings are social creatures, which means they follow others. That is why an empty restaurant will stay empty while hungry humans wait in line outside a crowded eatery. The ones in line believe they are waiting because they are hungry, but of course that's not the case. They wait because they want to be part of the crowd – because they follow leaders. More people get in line behind you. Now you are a leader. What do you want your followers to do? Hey guys, listen up! Let's go to that place on the other side of the street that's totally empty. Hey guys, listen up! Let's change the world; it's totally up to us!

Yoga. Yoga means union. If you are not alone, you are part of something bigger and understanding that everything is interconnected is crucial to our civilization. It's time to find leaders who see opportunities in union and collaboration, rather than in leaders who believe in isolation and conflict.

It is not true when people say: "We don't have enough resources or money." How many times throughout history has it been shown that wealth can grow into unimaginable and impossible quantities? Just think about the basics, like food. People are starving, but not because there is not enough food. In fact, about 40% of food produced is discarded. At the same time, millions suffer from diabetes, cancer and heart disease because they eat too much. People are starving and suffering from disease because there is no unity among the human race.

Future leaders understand that giving is the most rewarding strategy, simply because the greatest joy one can experience is the joy of helping others. They know that this mindset is the only sustainable solution to the challenges of our time, so they act out of generosity instead of fear. Today there are seven billion human beings sharing this one planet, so competition and conflict is not a sustainable strategy. And it's a losing strategy. In the hierarchical society, the goal was to reach the top, but in a network society there is no top. The goal is to have a big network, and the way to get there is by giving and by being united. The era of compassionate leaders is here, simply because anything else is impossible.

Yoga for leaders means union for people. If that is what you want, then this book is for you.

One more thing: You should not read this book with a critical mindset. There are numerous ways to interpret my words; I am wrong and I am right. But there is no right or wrong in yoga; being right is never the point. Read the text and let it seep into your own thoughts. Stop for a while, breathe and reflect. The purpose of yoga is to see things as they really are, without any distraction.

Read in.
Read out.

CHAPTER
ONE

THOUGHTS
ARE
DEADLY

*Your task is not to seek for love,
but merely to seek and find all
the barriers within yourself
that you have built against it.*

– Jalal al-Din Rumi

Maybe you never thought of trying yoga or meditation, but you probably have noticed the growing interest for ancient Eastern philosophy in today's Western society. The first part of this book will emphasize the relationship between spirituality and work life, and explain why this trend will continue to grow. I'll also provide exercises to help you practise stretching your mind and challenge your thinking. You will probably find some ideas that are very relevant in your current line of work, and some that might only provide inspiration to help you start thinking in new ways. The objective, however, is not to provide answers. The future is not a destination. My mission is to challenge your mind, make you ready for change and help you embrace it. The way you handle change will determine your success.

Change is the only thing constant in life, but the speed of change is something new. Human beings have 200,000 years of history but almost everything surrounding us in today is a result of change from the past 200 years. For thousands of years, life was very similar between generations and it was very important to pass on knowledge from generation to generation. That's not the case any longer. Our lives are completely different from the lives our parents lived, and our children will live very different lives than ours. Thus, experience might turn out to be useless. A graph with time on the x-axis and change on the y-axis looks like a perfect hockey-stick graph: change is currently riding the y-axis, straight up like a rocket launch (ever heard about "generation y"?).

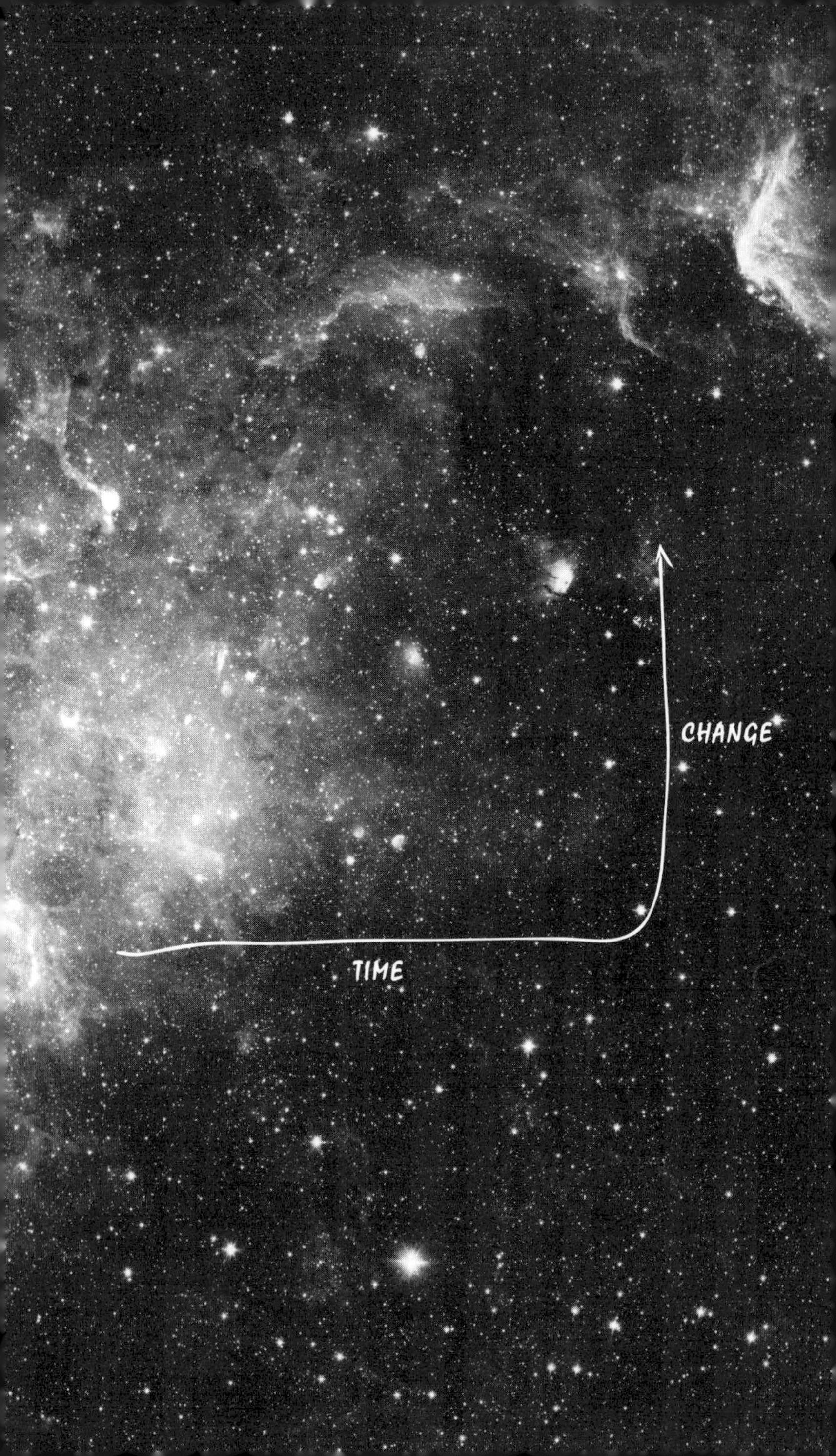
CHANGE
TIME

In this journey bound for the unknown and uncertain, it often feels like the world is spinning faster and faster, and even with our best intentions we can't keep up. This is a serious problem, because our brains like the illusion of control. In moments of extreme excitement, the human brain will produce a quick burst of epinephrine (adrenaline) and norepinephrine, which helps us think and act faster, and is potentially a life saver! But after adrenaline, the stressed brain will also release cortisol, a hormone that is helpful as long as too much of it is not released. Excess cortisol is linked to all the problems associated with chronic stress, lowered immune function, obesity, high blood pressure, insomnia, heart disease, brain fog, anxiety, depression, memory loss and others.

So chronic stress will eventually lead to illness. In many parts of the Western world, 90% of doctor visits are stress related. The World Health Organization says mental disorders will be the number-one health problem globally by 2030. Our greatest challenge is to alleviate stress and learn to live with change; to enjoy uncertainty.

There is nothing in this world more dangerous to you than your own thoughts. Therefore, it is safe to say that leaders – organizations, companies, brands, managers and others – who help others feel better will be the future winners.

To accomplish this, first you must go on the inward journey yourself.

CHAPTER TWO

THE TIME
IS ALWAYS
NOW

Go for it now. The future is promised to no one.

– Wayne Dyer

The future is often depicted as cyclic, which means trends come and go, everything is constantly changing, and it has all been seen before. But many trends of this era are disruptive, leading us to a future never imagined. Climate change, debt bubbles, uncontrolled migration, exponential technologies … no one has ever experienced the future facing us. As a result, much of what is "known" has become irrelevant. Experience might even be harmful. One sign of this is the life span among market-leading corporations. According to the current trends, 70% of today's Fortune 1,000 companies will not make the list ten years from now. Do an online search for "Fortune 1,000 companies" and look at the names; 700 of them will not be there if you check back in ten years' time.

So while the three-generation dilemma was often discussed in business – *wealth never survives three generations* – the important point and the most relevant observation of today is that leadership never survives a decade. Think about that for a second: thousands of old business models will be outperformed, millions of employees will have to find new jobs, and billions of invested dollars will be lost. Then think about all the companies that will be on the list in ten years. Many of them have not even been started yet, they are to be invented. Thousands of innovations, millions of jobs and billions of dollars to be won. This is the beginning; the beginning of this journey taking us to territories never before explored. And leadership doesn't survive a decade.

Climate change, debt bubbles, uncontrolled migration, exponential technologies ... no one has ever experienced the future facing us. As a result, much of what is "known" has become irrelevant.

On an individual level, this means that the work you do today will probably not be done – or at least not done the same way – in ten years' time.

When you think about change on a scale like this, you may feel negative stress, but you shouldn't. Remember the cortisol – it's not healthy for you. Negative thoughts and chronic stress are way more dangerous than smart competitors.

Think of it this way: change is great news for our future, considering how much still needs to be fixed. And you know from history that many things in life are actually much better today, even though at first people were very sceptical and stressed about change back then too. Secondly, humans are phenomenal at adapting, and have gone through so much challenging change during thousands of years. The problem is the speed. In a time of tech-revolution, change doesn't come gradually over years or generations; now it is more like a constant stream of Big Bangs. Problems that where always impossible to solve are suddenly solved and with that, everything in society changes right away. Steel can't fly, steel can't fly … BOOM! Wow … now steel can fly!

British science fiction author Douglas Adams gave us a set of rules that describes our reaction to technology. I believe that these can be used to understand our relationship with change:

1. Anything that is in the world when you're born is normal and ordinary and is just a natural part of the way the world works.

2. Anything that's invented when you're between 15 and 35 is new and exciting and revolutionary and you can probably have a career in it.

3. Anything invented after you're 35 is against the natural order of things.

In the next two decades, a tsunami of disruptive technologies and automation will diminish the amount of human work needed and will change the world economy as it is known today. Renewable energy will be much more efficient and cheaper to produce and store than fossil fuels. A transportation cloud of shared autonomous electric cars will solve congestion and pollution in metropolitan areas. Transactions will be verified by crypto currency and decentralized networks without big banks, and artificial intelligence and nano techology will change the rest of the world as we know it. These are just some examples and I will talk more about them later. The conclusion is obvious: no matter what one thinks about the future, it will be all about business as UNusual.

Our task is to adapt. With a smile.

Maybe you are among those who create change or maybe you are one of those waiting and watching others who push the existing boundaries and take risks. No matter who you are, everyone will have to adapt, and the cost for us to do so is obviously increasing. You pay attention, you follow the news, you absorb new trends, you check on what everybody else is up to. Everything seems to be so big, while as an individual you feel so small. What difference can one human make? Many of today's problems are big like this. It used to be important to grow everything big. Big is what everyone strives for: the bigger the better, big organizations, big products, big marketing, big bank accounts. Big beats small. But at a time when being fast is the key to success, big doesn't work anymore. Big is slow. Many of today's big organizations suffer from a growing disconnection with their customers, constant reorganization and an inability to innovate, while small companies with big networks are fast and close to all stakeholders. Fast is the new big. So big doesn't work, but the dying patient (big) is kept on life support because that seems easier than daring to face the consequence of death. How many times have we heard the phrase, "Too big to fail."?

But since nothing is fail-proof, the true definition of "too big to fail" is simply too big. Big problem!

This is why another big idea, big leader, or big solution is not the answer. Millions of ideas and leaders are required to attract billions of followers. One idea is yoga – to unite thinking and doing – and this book is one small contribution to create the new story of our amazing future. This future is often described as one of two main scenarios: utopia or dystopia. According to yoga philosophy, that is the wrong focus, simply because it is about a goal, something to be accomplished, rather than love of the action itself. Instead, try to think about your relationship with the present moment: "the now".

What is more important: the doing or the result of the doing? Do you treat this moment as an obstacle and do you feel you have a future moment to get to that is more important?

Read Eckhart Tolle's bestselling book, *The Power of Now*, if you'd like to go deeper on this topic and challenge your thinking.

The time is always now and the first step is awareness.

CHAPTER THREE

WHAT
ARISES
WILL
PASS

*Peace and negativity
cannot coexist,
just like light and
darkness cannot coexist.*

– S.N. Goenka

The population in the Western part of the world likes to simplify and put labels on complex things. To most people, yoga is associated with stretching exercises and physical activity, but the concept and meaning of yoga is much more. The Sanskrit word *yoga* means to unite. The union intended is when individuals – who have based their whole lives on the idea of being separated from others – realize that they are part of the wholeness; that everyone and everything is interconnected.

You think you are your body, which ends at the top of your fingers and toes. But the mother who gives birth to a child suddenly becomes two bodies, for a short time attached to each other through the umbilical cord. Is the child part of the mother after birth or are they separated in the moment the cord is cut? Is your fingernail part of you until you cut it and what is it then? What are you without it? Another person?

As a matter a fact, all cells in the entire body die and are replaced by new ones all the time. Your hair, your skin, your organs, everything is in a constant process of change. Find an old photograph of yourself and see: the change is striking. If the picture is 10, 20, or 30 years old, what you see is a totally different person from what you see in the mirror today.

The only thing left from the picture is your consciousness. You are aware of your existence, and this has made you believe in yourself as something isolated. But there is nothing in isolation. What would your life be like without everything you think of as outside of you, surrounding you? Imagine if all the people were gone, all living creatures, nature, all the trees, mountains, oceans, all the stuff, houses, cars, boats … everything gone. You are the only thing there is. What would that mean to the concept of you and your life? Disconnection is the result of your perception.

The purpose of yoga is enlightenment, a condition in which things are seen as they are without being affected by earlier experiences, opinions or reinterpretation.

We often believe in what we think. But our thoughts are just one version of the reality that shapes us and our actions, which means it is partly false. One example of this is that you can become sad just by thinking sad thoughts. Maybe the person next to you is thinking happy thoughts, smiling and chuckling at the same time you are suffering from anxiety. Same moment, same place, but two totally different realities.

All cells in the entire body die and are replaced by new ones all the time. Your hair, your skin, your organs, everything is in a constant process of change.

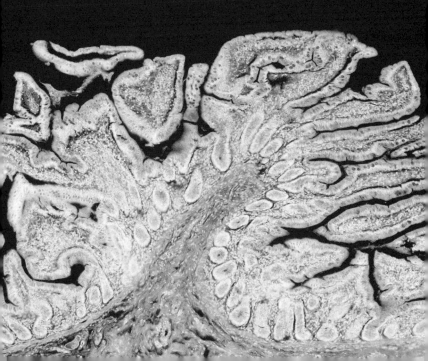

You wake up feeling great. The sun is shining and your breakfast is delicious. You pick up your phone and start scrolling: financial crisis, terror and death, a new disease discovered. The great feeling is gone, even though nothing actually happened except in your mind. You had a good night's sleep, the sun is still shining and breakfast is tasty, but your thoughts changed and so did your reality.

You do this to yourself all the time.

Your boss calls for an urgent meeting, you feel a strange ache in your chest, you receive a cryptic text message from your child's friend … with a little help from your imagination you are convinced of a terrible reality and it is impossible to enjoy the moment. Later on, you realize that you were wrong. The meeting with your boss was positive, the ache in your body is gone, and your child's friend simply happened to text the wrong number.

This is seen with time, as well. Your mind is a time machine, constantly trying to lure you with exotic trips to everywhere but now. You go back in time to thresh and re-experience – Why didn't I say that … Oh, those were the days – and you travel to the future to worry and dream (Maybe I'll fail … What if I win …) Of course, the present moment contains everything yesterday and tomorrow can offer, but you don't see that because you are seduced by time travelling. How many present moments do you miss like this because you are in another time?

The Yoga Sutras of Patanjali* describes the vision of yoga: "Yoga Chitta Vritti Nirodha," which means to stop identifying with our thoughts. Imagine if you could actually do that – take a few steps backwards and watch yourself like you watch others. Am I angry now? Did I become angry just because that other motorist cut in front of me without signalling? Interesting – I didn't know I was short-tempered. Am I an aggressive person or is it just today? Am I out of balance or is it habitual? Am I always irritated when I drive? The guy who cut in front of me is gone; maybe he is happy. For how long am I going to be angry?

The power of your thoughts is monstrous. They will make your mouth dry, your body shiver, your pulse and breath become uncontrolled. Blush, laughter, tears, shudder, sexual arousal … you can get goosebumps just by thinking of nails being scraped on a chalkboard.

Some mental exercises try to help you disconnect from negative thoughts, but yoga is all about the opposite: to calm your mind to see the world for what it is and recognize reality as it is. Yoga helps us stop pretending that everything is the way we'd like it to be.

This is important, because we never experience the alternative to what is happening (what would have happened if what happened hadn't happened?) and even more so because reality is relative. One person's dream is another person's nightmare. Two people can look at the same man and see a jerk or a tender romantic. Time and culture are also a great example on the liquidity of reality. Today, thoughts that used to be punished by death are admired, and people seen as heroes in one culture are condemned by another. This is also true in the world of business: what one company tries to accomplish, another company tries to avoid. One team celebrates, one is distressed. One company just starting, while another one files for bankruptcy. It's not good or bad – it just is. Humans die because they are born, that doesn't mean birth is bad.

Last summer I participated in Vipassana meditation training. The course is rather strict, and it is performed the exact same way all over the world. Participants spend ten days in total silence, practicing meditation from wake-up at 4am to bedtime at 9pm. Lodging and food is simple and there is no access to external stimulus such as media or social interaction. You are not even allowed to bring a pen and paper.

The setup is designed this way in order for the participants to get far away from daily distractions so that they can start to observe themselves more objectively. If you've ever tried meditation, you know how hard it is to refrain from drifting away in the sea of thoughts, constantly offered by the time machine of your mind. And, of course, I experienced hours of totally worthless meditation during my ten days. But I also learned the concept of not evaluating. In every moment, there is suffering and joy. Sitting still without moving your legs, arms and back, completely focused on your bodily sensations for one hour straight will make you realize that this is true. Everything is in a constant mode of change. Some people will object and say that some things – like a stone or a mountain – do not change, but you know they do, it's just a matter of time. Everything in the universe is in a constant mode of change.

The *Pāli* word – the sacred language of Buddhism – for impermanence is *anicca*, the Buddhist notion that the existence of all conditions, without exception, is transient or in a constant state of flux. Therefore permanence – to keep something – is nothing but an illusion. What arises will pass.

* Yoga Sutras of Patanjali: yoga systemized as a philosophy a couple of hundred years before Christ.

CHAPTER FOUR

BREATH
IS THE
BRIDGE

*When the breath wanders,
the mind also is unsteady.
But when the breath is calmed,
the mind too will be still, and
the yogi achieves long life.
Therefore, one should learn
to control the breath.*

– Hatha Yoga Pradipika

Did you ever forget where you left the car keys, what someone else just said, what you were supposed to buy in the grocery store? People do all sorts of things on autopilot. They often think about something completely different than that which is actually going on in the present moment. Think about when you have been really distracted; sometimes you may have found you went on for weeks without noticing your surroundings. When you act without awareness, you are like a sleepwalker: your mind controls you. You are somewhere else.

The secret of awareness is to watch everything that is going on right now. To master your mind, you need to watch what is going on inside of your body and mind, as a witness, and breath is the most accessible tool to do this. The reason breathing is so powerful is because it affects your physical state and you can do it consciously as well as unconsciously. When you are sleeping, your body is breathing without any need for you to think about it, just like your organs are always working without you thinking about them. But when thinking about your breathing, you can also control it, by holding your breath or by breathing faster and so on. You cannot do this with organs like your liver or your heart. If I tell you to feel your kidney or lower your blood pressure, you can't. But if I tell you to breathe faster you can, and thereby you can manipulate your physical state of breathing. You have probably witnessed someone faint as a result of hyperventilation, and you have definitely felt how a couple of deep breaths can be calming when stressed.

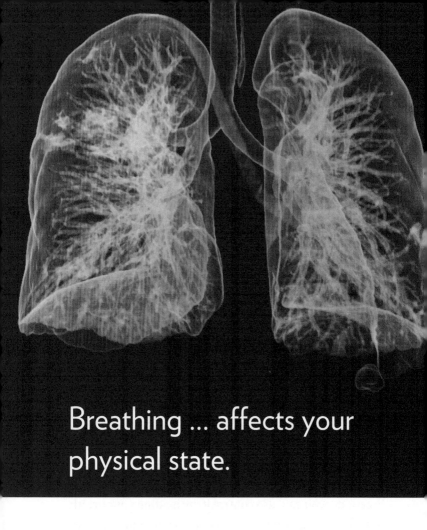

Breathing ... affects your physical state.

Any time you feel a disconnection, when stress is building up inside of you, when your mind is in total control and thoughts are negative, conscious breathing will be the bridge that unifies body and mind. In these cases, you need to take a step back and watch yourself in total awareness.

Breathing exercises are a great habit that will help you be more present, more focused and more aware. And best of all, they can be done any time, anywhere.

Sit up straight in comfortable position. Close your eyes and focus on your breathing. Breathe through your nose, slightly deeper than normal. Be aware of your breath, the feeling when it comes in through the nostrils, filling your lungs and belly, and passing out again. When you notice that you are thinking of something else, acknowledge that thought and let it move on. Turn back your focus to your breathing. If you never practised meditation before, this is very challenging. A mantra can be of help if you feel too distracted; you can count every inhalation and exhalation, like counting sheep to fall asleep. Or you can even start to think about the air that is passing in and out of you. Inhale – where did this air come from? Maybe it travelled over oceans and mountains from other parts of the world and right now it is passing through you. Maybe the person next to you just had parts of the air you are breathing in her lungs. That means parts of her are parts of you now. Exhale – now parts of you move on to somewhere else. Breathing is key to yoga, even if you are doing asanas (specific postures). The point is not to stretch and bend like an Instagram-acrobat, but to actually feel a connection between the body and the mind; to feel a union.

Breathing is the bridge that unites.

CHAPTER FIVE

COUNT DOWN

If you change the way you look at things, the things you look at change.

– Wayne Dyer

Earth formed more than 4.6 billion years ago and more than 99% of all species that ever lived on this planet are estimated to be extinct.

There were five mass extinctions, when more than 75% of species disappeared during a relatively short period of time, events that nearly ended life on Earth. One was "the great dying" 251 million years ago, when 96% of species disappeared. Among the few survivors from that time was the reptile cynodont, which means "dog teeth". It was about the size of a rat, with sharp teeth to catch small arthropods and crush their shells. The body of cynodonts evolved over each generation, providing a little better insulation to keep a steady body temperature during cold nights, better sense of smell and hearing, and so on. To be able to manage all of these sensitive senses, the brain of the cynodont grew in size through the generations. Today, the offspring of cynodonts have elephant trunks, hoofs and smartphones. They are the ancestors of all mammals, including human beings.

More than 150 years ago, Charles Darwin introduced the evolution theory, which taught us that survival was never about being bigger, stronger, faster or smarter, but about the ability to adapt to change. You and I are here because our forefathers managed to change. History proves that humans are great at adapting to all sorts of change. The ability to manage all kinds of situations and conditions is our strongest and most distinguished feature.

Earth formed more than 4.6 billion years ago and more than 99% of all species that ever lived on this planet are estimated to be extinct.

The problem with humans and change is the illusion of permanence. When we believe we can keep something, we believe in control and thus fear change, since the outcome is unknown.

But remember, what arises will pass. Nothing is permanent.

A couple years ago, I met with Swedish elite swimmer Christoffer Lindhe. At the age of 17, Christoffer was run over by a freight train; he survived but lost both of his legs and his left arm. Because of his training and being in good shape as an athlete, his heart managed to keep pumping, despite having lost a lot of blood and having very little blood left in his body. Imagine the feeling of waking up to that – three of your limbs are gone.

How often do you think about your legs and arms? But if parts of your body were no longer there, would you wake up as another person?

Almost exactly two years after the terrible accident, Christoffer was back in the blocks, swimming in the Beijing Paralympics. Today he has won several Swedish championship gold medals, a bronze in the European championships, and three bronze medals in the World Cup. Christoffer didn't just survive; he is among the best in the world.

There are many stories of people who managed extreme challenges, accidents that mutilated their bodies, horrific concentration camps, natural disasters and people that lost everything – stories that make you wonder how it's even possible to go on. But evidently it is. Human beings are capable of dealing with situations far worse than they believe are possible.

Our ability to adapt is one of our greatest powers.

What if adaptability is just like any other strength, and you can become stronger and better with practise and exercise? Just like going to the gym to exercise your muscles, maybe you should give the 'change muscle' a workout every now and then. Quit your job and get a new one! Go for a new career, meet new people, talk to people who don't agree with you, travel to different places and study seemingly strange behaviours, listen with the intention to understand rather than to debate, go out in the wild and live from nature, or when facing two choices pick the one that feels uncertain. It doesn't even have to be a big thing to become life changing. Try small changes to daily routines, like how you get to work: if you normally use the metro, switch and cycle for a month; your life will become richer just by adding change. And you will become fearless.

If you don't do this, you will gradually become weaker and weaker, and thus have a hard time adapting to even small changes. That's why older people often are considered conservative. Remember Douglas Adams: "Anything invented after you're 35 seems against the natural order of things."

And don't use time as an excuse – you have time. As a matter of fact, time is all you have. Those who do not find time for exercise now will have to find time for illness later.

This is also true when thinking about your ability to adapt to change. The more you exercise, the stronger you will get and you will feel an increased confidence in your own ability. Self-confidence is one of the greatest strengths, and it will help you feel security in a time where you know the speed of change is increasing and uncertainty is the only certainty. Trust in one's own ability beats any amount of money in a bank account.

Of course, Christoffer Lindhe wouldn't have chosen his destiny if he'd had the option, even though he ended up being one of the best in the world. I am not trying to offer advice like "quit your job" or "change this and that today". Other people's lifestyle and choices might not suit you. The point is to emphasize the fact that no one can escape change, but everyone can learn how to feel better about it. Only you can determine at what level you are and where you want to go.

I am 45 at the time I write this, and statistically if I don't have an accident or anything like that, I have 35 more years to do something meaningful with my life. Next year that will be 34 years. To me it is illogical to count upward from my birthday, as that will create the illusion of eternal life. I want to do the opposite; to remind myself that time is limited: 35, 34, 33, 32 … I'm not afraid of dying, but I'm terrified of not living when I have the chance.

Exercise your ability to adapt to change and count down.

CHAPTER SIX

BEAT
YOURSELF

You cannot do yoga.
Yoga is your natural state.
What you can do are yoga
exercises, which may reveal
to you where you are resisting
your natural state.

– Sharon Gannon

In business, people often talk about change as a process, with a beginning and an end. "We are in a reorganization, it will be done by the end of August, then we're good to go again." Forget about ever being done. Change is constant; what arises will pass.

Great leaders understand that they have been successful when they are no longer needed. The worst managers make sure the whole organization is totally dependent on their presence. They think of themselves as decision makers and thus believe they should be involved in every decision and control as much as possible. But the objective for any organization is to become efficient, and a manager who is self-centered will create the opposite. A great metaphor is parenthood. The objective of any parent is to foster a child's independence. At times, a child will be on the wrong track and need directing, but essentially parenting is about support and patience and no matter how scary it feels, eventually every parent has to let go.

Great leaders are like parents. They don't always know what's best for their organizations and sometimes they feel insecure and scared about letting go. But their ambition is to make their organization strong and to create independence.

Many large organizations suffer from self-centered managers who focus more time and energy on the organization itself, and the hierarchy within, rather than the output they should be trying to create. Managers as controllers were born in the industrial era, when workers were hired to do what they were told and not to think for themselves. Workers were to be managed. In today's knowledge economy, this is totally illogical and counterproductive. Today you want thinkers, not just workers. You want employees to bring engagement and creativity to work, not only a pair of hands for the assembly line like in the old days. If you put effort into finding and attracting smart people, and then remove their intelligence and responsibility, you will have missed the whole point.

A new trend is the no-manager approach. One example of this is seen in Holacracy, a fluid organizational structure in which individuals have high authority to make decisions and teams are self-organized. According to Holacracy.org, more than 300 organizations already use and work with a Holacracy approach, which "removes power from management hierarchy and distributes it across clear roles". Another example that can give you a hint of future leadership philosophy is "paid paid vacation" introduced by FullContact (a US-based tech company) CEO Bart Lorang. Once per year the company offers its employees 7,500 USD to go on vacation; the only rule to follow is to disconnect totally. They are not allowed to work, not even allowed to check their e-mails once, while on vacation. This will be visited again later in the book.

A hint of future leadership philosophy is paid paid vacation.

Great people will be attracted by independence and will contribute with innovation and creativity only when leaders understand that their task is to support rather than to control.

It's very important to have a true understanding of the problems you solve. This is where our focus as leaders should be. Maybe you don't think of yourself as a problem-solver, but you are. As a leader, you are constantly in a "look-for-problems-and-think-about-solutions mode". At work you get paid to solve problems (if you don't solve a problem, no one will pay you). Sometimes the problem being solved is referred to as customers' needs. By focusing on your customers' needs rather than the solution you provide, it will be easier to come up with better solutions – faster, cheaper, more efficient ones. Ultimately you might be able to challenge yourself and think about how to solve the problem in a different way. How would you solve it if you started today, from zero? Is there a better way to serve customers if you start from scratch? This is what entrepreneurship is all about: new solutions that will destroy old business models.

Sometimes you hear managers talk about disruptive innovation, entrepreneurship and new business models in a way that makes it sound as though they would like these things, but think again. Pretend you are my boss and I walk into your office with great enthusiasm to tell you how to kill our own business model. Do you believe any successful manager or organization actually would like that? Well, they should. Next generation leaders will!

Our greatest fear should not be of failure, but of succeeding at things in life that don't really matter. The goal is to beat yourself. If you don't do it, someone else will.

CHAPTER
SEVEN

BEWARE
THE RISK OF
IGNORANCE

Before you've practised,
the theory is useless.
After you've practised,
the theory is obvious.

– David Williams

As a public speaker, people often tell me that they already understand the speed of change, that it's not necessary to talk about it. But change in today's world is many times exponential, not linear, so I don't think anyone understands the speed and what is actually ahead of us. As human beings, we think in terms of what we can relate to and often base our expectations on experience.

If I were to tell you that I'm going to take 30 steps and ask you to predict the future, you would respond by pointing out my finish line, at about 30 meters away. This is what you can relate to. This is linear.

If I were to tell you that I'm going to take 30 exponential steps, it would be much harder to predict where I'm going to end up. Ok, you understand what exponential means in theory. Each step in an exponential trend is double the previous, so 1, 2, 4, 8, 16, 32. While this is kind of unusual, the conclusion is even more confusing. Each exponential step is equal to the total progress of all previous steps, so the last step is the half-way point and therefor we're always at the knee of the curve. Therefore, if I took 30 exponential steps toward my finish line, this would be a billion meters away; that is, 26 times around the planet. One more step would be 52 times around the world. This is exponential.

Many of today's business models and products are a result of the exponential trend in processing power.

You have probably heard the term "Moore's law". In 1965, the founder of the tech company Intel, Gordon Moore, published a paper explaining his observation that the number of transistors in a microchip doubles every year. Gordon also made a prediction that this exponential trend would continue for at least a decade. In 1975, he revised the forecast to doubling every two years. Moore's law is an observation and not a natural law, but the prediction proved accurate for several decades and many of today's business models and products are a result of the exponential trend in processing power.

One well-known example is Kodak. I am not going to tell you the story of stupid managers and the lack of innovation, but rather the opposite. Eastman Kodak Company was the world leader in photography for more than 130 years, known for pioneering technology and innovative marketing. With almost 90% of the market share in film and cameras, Kodak was referred to as "the Google of its day". Kodak products were on the moon! So let's not fool ourselves and buy into the easy story of lack of innovation.

Steve Sasson, the inventor of the world's first digital camera, was a Kodak employee, so the company was in fact a pioneer in digital-photo technology as well. But as always with technology, the first versions were not very convincing. The digital camera Steve presented in 1975 weighed 3.6kg/8lbs and took 23 seconds to record one 0.01 megapixel black-and-white image to be played back on a television screen. It is easy to understand why this was not very impressive to any of Steve's managers. Kodak was a brand associated with quality, razor-sharp pictures and beautiful colors, so 0.01 megapixels was obviously not relevant, and who would want to watch photographs on a screen? "Kodak moments" were framed and hung a wall.

However – and this is key to the story – Steve told his managers that digital technology would evolve very rapidly and probably be good enough to compete with film in just 15 years. This prediction turned out to be correct almost to the date, and in the early 1990s several camera manufacturers introduced digital SLR-cameras with 1.3 megapixel sensors, and the quality of digital photos was starting to look like film. The rest is history and so is Kodak, which tried to protect its existing business model instead of disrupting it.

It's easy to understand why Steve Sasson was arguing for the importance of technology; most engineers do. But how did he know it was going to take 15 years?

You know the answer by now. Steve knew about Moore's law.

Kodak was referred to as
"the Google of its day."

So let's assume we are back in 1975. You are the CEO of Kodak, with 90% market share. Last year you sold millions of cameras. Now one of your employees, a 24-year-old tech guy who just demonstrated the worst product you ever saw, tells you that the global market for this might be billions of cameras, thousands of times more than your existing business. People will take a trillion photographs per year. This clearly can't happen with 24- or 36-exposure film rolls that have to be developed and printed on paper.

So what do you do? You are the world leader, with 145,000 employees. With that responsibility, you have to focus on margins and return on investment (ROI) before you decide how to allocate resources. Everyone loves to hear the stories of entrepreneurs and cowboy-leaders, but as any organization grows it prefers stability and the illusion of control. So managers in big companies are there simply because they are *not* daredevils.

The true definition of ROI in the 21st century is "risk of ignorance." Instead of referring to Kodak as a "they-missed-it" example, it should be addressed as the first great example of a digitally disrupted company. Let's use it to understand how hard, or almost impossible, it is when disruption from exponential technologies comes knocking on your door.

Right now this is happening in many huge industries, such as the automotive industry. (More on this in a later chapter). Tech companies like Tesla, Uber, Google and Apple are entering the market, and even though old leaders talk about how they will try to disrupt themselves with projects focused on ride-sharing and self-driving cars, I would not bet my money on Ford, GM, Toyota or VW. My prediction is that most of today's leaders will go the Kodak way. The reason for this is explained in the book *The Innovator's Dilemma* by Clayton Christensen: "In our studies of this challenge, we have never seen a company succeed in addressing a change that disrupts its mainstream values absent the personal, attentive oversight of the CEO."

And oversight is not enough, to succeed, the CEO will have to work hard, with the ambition to kill his own business model. Leaders are being disrupted not because they are bad, but because they are good at what they do. If you try to disrupt within a big company, the organizational immune system will come to get you.

Kodak didn't die because they were bad. Kodak died because they were the best at doing what no one wants anymore.

CHAPTER
EIGHT

IT IS (ALWAYS) THE BEST AND WORST OF TIMES

We are the first generation to feel the impact of climate change, and the last generation that can do something about it.

– Barack Obama

Warfare, disease, poverty and infant mortality are at record lows, and freedom, democracy, education and longevity are at all-time highs. In many parts of the world, average people enjoy a standard of living that surpasses that of mid-19th century kings and queens. Never before in history has life been this good for so many human beings. But for everything that is not human, it has never been worse. While the exact total number of species in existence is not yet known (scientists discover new ones all the time), what is known for certain – pollution, land conversion and climate change – is ground for a very serious biodiversity crisis. Planet Earth's ecosystems are in a bad shape and the growing consumption of resources is not sustainable.

Negative effects are not only obvious in poor countries where floods, droughts, lack of clean water and disease are part of daily life. Social, political, ecological and economic instability, growing numbers of refugees and heavy pollution, are examples of the daily news in the developed world of the 21st century. As I'm writing this, Beijing just issued its second "red alert" of the year for hazardous air pollution. The 20-million-plus inhabitants of the modern megacity have been advised to stay indoors, restricted from using their cars, schools are closed, and construction sites have shut down. And as a tragicomic manifestation of the unsustainable era, the Canadian company Vitalityair offers wealthy Beijingers crisp mountain air in a bottle. No mistake about the vision for our future – no money, no air.

Pollution, land conversion and climate change – is ground for a very serious biodiversity crisis.

To the ignorant, this just means that others are in trouble: other species, other countries, other people. They ignore the fact that everyone is interconnected, so they ignore the problem until they themselves are in trouble. When Canada has to issue a red alert for polluted air and no money in the world can buy a clean last breath, then it is too late. Luckily the "climate deniers" are one of the dying species. A majority of people understand that our relation to nature unites all humans, no matter what nationality, ethnicity or religion. We are all citizens of planet Earth and there is no business on a dead planet.

While the rich lives that have resulted from the industrial era, free market capitalism and globalization are very much acknowledged and appreciated, it is understood that this is a one-way road. Whatever used to work in a world with one billion people isn't going to work now when there are seven billion of us. A narrow-minded focus on money isn't necessarily great for future wealth, and nationalism and protectionism will only lead to isolation and stagnation in a networked society. Citizens of the world demand a shift; just look at politics, where voters are attracted by everything anti-establishment, and the extreme position is to resist change and protect the status quo. Ordinary people have lost faith; they don't believe established leaders are capable of solving ordinary problems. To quote American journalist and author Chris Hedges: "We now live in a nation where doctors destroy health, lawyers destroy justice, universities destroy knowledge, governments destroy freedom, the press destroys information, religion destroys morals and our banks destroy the economy." Life has never been better to so many before, but a shift is necessary from short-term, unsustainable egoism to long-term, sustainable collectivism.

CHAPTER
NINE

A DYSFUNCTIONAL SYSTEM

This yoga is not possible,
for the one who eats too much,
or does not eat at all,
who sleeps too much,
or who keeps awake.

– Bhagavad Gita

Climate crisis, refugee crisis, food crisis … no matter what problem you focus on, it will very quickly become a problem about money and limited resources. The same thing happens in your personal life: most problems tend to come down to money. This is why so many people believe that money would make them happy – more on that later.

Economy is from the Greek words "οίκος", meaning household and "νέμομαι", meaning manage. It refers to the understanding of how to manage our household. So let's define our household: there are currently 7.5 billion people on one planet growing at about 1.2 million people each week (births minus deaths). According to demographic experts, there will be ten billion people on the planet by the year 2050.

To manage this household – of seven billion people growing to ten billion – it is crucial to define what resources are required and the limitations ahead. According to Maslow's hierarchy of needs (a psychological theory proposed by Abraham Maslow), there are five levels of needs that are shared by everyone: physiological (water, food, warmth); safety (security, health); love (friends, sex); esteem (prestige, respect); and self-actualization (creativity, acceptance of facts).

Maslow never mentioned money. But a working system is necessary. With a great system, people can be incentivized to collaborate and give priority to important problems. So far two main tracks have been tried: socialism and capitalism.

However, with the collapse of the Berlin Wall and the Soviet Union, the world came to agree that socialism doesn't work. But the great wall of capitalism is still standing, undisputed and heavily guarded. Today's gatekeepers – the national central banks and their presidents, who do not look like the military at Checkpoint Charlie – have faith in a system they want to protect. And just like back in the days of the Cold War, they are willing to do whatever it takes to defend it.

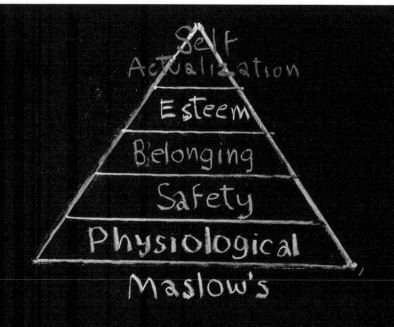

For more than a decade now, the (developed) world economy has been in a constant need for stimulus to be able to grow. More than 20 national central banks have lowered interest rates to zero, or below, and when that didn't work they initiated money printing programs – quantitative easing (QE) – which instead adds to the public debt. The objective is said to be economic growth, but unfortunately the only thing growing is debt with a bonus of environmental problems and depression among the people trapped inside the wall. The cure seems to be worse than the actual problem, but still there is no sign of doubt in the system.

A 2015 report by McKinsey Global Institute, *Debt and (Not Much) Deleveraging**, examines the evolution of debt across 47 countries. "Since the great recession, global debt has grown by $57 trillion, outpacing the world gross domestic product (GDP) growth and no major economy has decreased its debt-to-GDP ratio since 2007. That poses new risks to financial stability."

The reason for having a centralized banking system, a boss, is to maintain control, but no one knows where the zero-interest-rate policy will take us. It has never been tried before. Interest rates have been previously used to price risk, but the risk-pricing mechanism has now been broken. It is now commonly known that when we talk about economic growth, we are actually talking about lending and spending today, what needs to be grown and paid in the future.

Central bankers have lost control. To say this is not to say that socialism was a better system. It is simply to say that capitalism isn't working in a developed world where populations have stopped growing. A better system is needed.

This notion is not only growing among millennials from the Occupy movement, but also in the elite of the World Economic Forum, where topics such as inequality are among current top priorities. Consumers (the market) used to get purchasing power from salaries, but as a result of increased free trade (globalization) and automation (information technology), income in the developed world has stagnated for millions of workers. When I grew up in the 1970s, one income was enough to support a family; today a family often runs on two incomes, plus maximum debt. Maybe that alone is enough to explain weak growth. Today's consumers are shopping on credit.

A consumer-based economy needs consumers with purchasing power; if consumers are poor or broke, the market will not thrive.

Food is another good example that shows that capitalism doesn't work well globally. People are starving, but isn't there enough food to feed the whole household of humanity? As you know, the true answer is that there is enough food, the problem is that it is very badly distributed. The ones who are not hungry have more than enough, so they throw away 40% of the food produced and still have too much to eat and therefore die from heart disease and other illnesses. So while half of the household is dying of hunger, the other half is dying of obesity. A lose-lose situation.

Can anyone defend such a dysfunctional system? Oh yes, people who are stuck in ideology can, and they do. Fundamentalists act deaf and blind, not interested in dialogue, to listen, understand and learn. They like to debate, to argue and explain why they are right and others are wrong. Criticism of capitalism is synonymous to support for socialism; it's red or blue, left or right. Right? To make things worse, this is exactly what the mainstream media loves: conflict! A right and a wrong.

The greatest obstacle, however, comes from the winners, the ones on top of the wall. With money comes power and why would they use this power to step away from the current system and support a new system? People are working eight hours a day to pay interest on the money they owe. Private banks and the financial industry make money like no one ever dreamed of throughout history, by inflating these enormous debt bubbles.

The simple fact that banking is the most profitable business of all should be enough to make everyone suspicious. What does a bank do? Think about it. How does a bank create value?

There is enough food, the problem is that it is very badly distributed.

Maybe it is easier to flip the question and ask it from the other side: What problems would be solved, what values would be created, if everybody worked in banking?

If you ask the guards of the capitalistic wall, they will explain they deserve obscene profits because of the risk associated with lending. But as you know, they don't risk anything. They don't have the money to lend; there is not a bank on Earth that can pay its debts. Remember this next time you check your online bank balance. That number is just how much the bank owes you; it's not like they have a pile of cash with your name on it stashed away in a vault somewhere.

The last time that there were long queues of people outside closed ATMs was when Cyprus's financial system imploded in the spring of 2013, but do you remember any pictures of jailed bankers? No, the islands of political leaders were forced to sign a bailout deal or watch the banking system collapse. Capitalism for profits and socialism for losses. The banks never lose; they don't risk anything.

But banks are covered by assets; they don't lend without securities, some may object. Well, banks are lending money that doesn't exist against assets (stocks, homes, salaries, etc.), as if those assets are definite. But nothing is definite. Stock markets go down, housing bubbles are bursting, and employees can become unemployed. Then the only thing left is debt.

When markets are going up no one wants to be a party pooper, but when they turn down it's all panic. At the time of writing this book, the Shanghai stock exchange is falling dramatically. To stop the negative trend, it is stopping trade when stocks go below -7%. Two years ago, when stocks were up 150%, there was no talk about stopping anything.

This debt system is forcing us to hunt for fast growth; without it, people won't be able to pay interest on the money they borrowed yesterday. The question is whether today's capitalistic system will fail like socialism, because of its own dysfunctionality, or be challenged by a better working system.

I don't believe the revolution is far away, but it's probably not you and me who will start it. Almost three billion people in the world don't have a bank account. On the other side of our wall is the developing world. They don't have a system to protect.

* http://www.mckinsey.com/global-themes/employment-and-growth/debt-and-not-much-deleveraging

CHAPTER
TEN

THE IDEA
OF
MONEY

No one is wise by birth.
Wisdom results from
one's own efforts.

– **Tirumalai Krishnamacharya**

On the small island of Yap in the Pacific Ocean, people use stones as money. The stone-currency is called Rai and most of the stones are shaped like donuts with holes in the center. One Rai stone can be anything between a small eight-centimeter piece to four meters in diameter. Many Rai are from other islands as far away as New Guinea, more than 1,000 kilometers from Yap. The value of each Rai is determined by the stone's size and history; most of the stones are so big that it takes 20 people to move them, so Rai is not a currency one can easily carry around. Your Rai is where you left it, but that doesn't matter as long as everyone knows who the owner of each stone is.

One of the stones included in Yap's economy is not even on the island; it fell overboard during a dramatic expedition many years ago and is located on the ocean floor. But crew members who survived the storm told everyone about the stone and the people of Yap trust the story, although few have seen the stone. The owner of the stone on the bottom of the ocean is a very rich man.

On the small island of Yap in the Pacific Ocean, people use stones as money.

Money is just an idea on how to preserve value and purchasing power. In the beginning, stones, shells and precious metals were used to trade for goods. But today most societies have adapted from gold coins to paper money to digital money. But to believe in the idea of digital money is probably as strange as to believe in stones on the bottom of an ocean. Try using your plastic card in a rural village and see for yourself. The only thing important to money is trust. The system is based on trust and the value of a currency is dependent on trust in the issuers' ability to pay their debt. When people start to question the issuers' ability to pay their debt, a currency will fall.

In the trading days, a farmer offered a hunter a bag of wheat in exchange for a piece of meat. The hunter was better at acquiring meat and the farmer was better at acquiring wheat; a win-win-deal. The problem with a barter system is that you often need to consume your goods immediately. You cannot wait a month to eat the piece of meat you traded for, and if the farmer didn't want meat but fish, the system didn't work for either one.

Using precious metals to preserve buying power presented a much more flexible way of trading. By using coins people could save, and since the availability of gold and silver does not increase overnight, the value was more reliable. As people chose to keep their gold in a safe place rather than to carry it around, goldsmiths became the start of the modern banking system in 1700s in London. At the insertion, the owner got a receipt that entitled them to charge the same amount at a later time, and soon people began trading with receipts and paper money was born.

So instead of bringing a sack of gold to trade, which the seller would have to deposit immediately, it was enough to hand over a receipt. The seller could easily verify with the issuer of the receipt that it was genuine and that the gold was there to collect at any time. It wasn't long before the goldsmiths realized that depositors never wanted to collect their gold. They figured out that they could print more receipts than the gold they actually had, and in this way they were able to increase profitability by charging interest rates. Hence, the banknote system of today began, and the principle was based on having trust in the bank.

Up until 1971, the US dollar was linked to gold. Until the 70s, you could actually go to a bank to withdraw your money in gold. But as President Nixon's Vietnam War dragged on and ate into the state budget, he chose to break the so-called Bretton Woods Agreement, which said that the exchange value of the dollar was guaranteed with gold. The new solution was fiat currency. Fiat is Latin for "let it be done", which basically means that the United States government guarantees the value of the dollar.

The US is the world's largest economy; the world's oil is traded in US dollars and so most major economies use the dollar as their reserve currency. But the US national debt is $19 trillion and climbing. On any dollar bill, you can read the words "legal tender", which means that it is determined by law that the dollar will be legal tender, regardless of what happens. But you can also read the words "In God we trust." So maybe in the end it's not a bank or a state, but God we all have to trust. Close your eyes and think about that for a minute.

Fiat currencies have actually been around since the beginning of civilization. Marco Polo told about the Song and Ming dynasties dealing with paper money backed by state guarantee. All fiat currencies that ever existed have one thing in common: they eventually collapsed because the state inflated the currency by printing too much money.

Coins in the Roman Empire were initially 95% silver, but as confidence in the empire increased, emperors chose to issue coins with minor silver content. In the end, the silver content of a denarius coin was 0.5% and inflation went up 1,000% in 15 years. The value of money fell like a stone (not a Rai) and contributed to the final collapse.

After the First World War, German banknotes were worth more as fuel for the fireplace than as currency. And the same situation occurred in Zimbabwe, one of

Africa's richest countries in 2003, where shops began using slates to write prices because they often multiplied during the course of a day. The Zimbabwe hyperinflation peaked at 231 million per cent in 2008 and in 2009 the Zimbabwe dollar was abandoned as the local currency and all local debt was wiped out. Since the Nixon debacle during the Vietnam War, central banks have come to control the economy, with the task of accelerating and breaking free from the influence of desperate politicians. But ever since the last debt bubble in 2008, the Western world has suffered from a stagnant economy, in constant need of life support.

Money is and will remain a way to preserve purchasing power. But any real value, like something you can eat, has long since been abandoned.

One more problem is the fact that almost all the money in today's system is not issued by a central bank, but by private banks. Since everything went digital, they never need to pay us anything, so they really just fudge around in a huge numbers game. Every time they issue a credit, new "money" is created and they can charge interest. If the economy is growing, one might think the amount of debt will be reduced, but unfortunately in today's financial system money is created by adding debt.

The system is based on lending fictitious money. Try to explain that to the people of Yap.

CHAPTER ELEVEN

POWER
TO THE
PEOPLE

Have only love in your heart for others. The more you see the good in them, the more you will establish good in yourself.

– **Paramahansa Yogananda**

A concentration of power has always been a problem. A person, an organization, a political party or a corporation will, as they accumulate power, eventually start to abuse it. History is full of great ambitions turned into dictatorship. Left, right, freedom fighter, entrepreneur … it doesn't matter, everybody has good intentions from the beginning and the transition comes gradually with power.

It is not necessary to use examples like the North Korean dictator Kim Jong-un; the democratic world is full of leaders who lost their connection to reality and a remotely normal life. Sepp Blatter, president of the international football association (FIFA) for 17 years, was forced to resign and is currently being investigated for corruption and criminal activities. Kenneth Lay, the son of a priest, who worked his way to the top and founded one of the world's largest energy companies, was convicted of fraud. According to *Fortune* magazine, his creation, Enron, was "the most innovative company in the US" but it turned out that the innovation was in its bookkeeping and financial reports. The investigation that led to the collapse of Enron, and left thousands of employees without a job or retirement savings, proved that Lay and his partner in crime, Jeffrey Skilling, played God and manipulated the California energy grid by turning the power off when they wanted a better position in negotiations.

A recent example of the problem is Volkswagen, led by chairman Martin Winterkorn, who was caught manipulating 11 million cars during six years to pass emissions tests by cheating. One of the world's leading automakers had been emitting 40 times more nitrogen oxide in real-world driving than showed when tested, and the fraud was done just to keep investors happy. The scandal has so far led to the biggest financial loss in the company's history. More important are the environmental harm and the loss of lives as a result of polluted air.

The people in the center of a centralized system will eventually corrupt the system entirely to serve their own needs as they accumulate power and control. That has always been the case throughout history. So maybe the strange thing is that we are surprised and upset when hearing about these scandals. And it's even stranger that we still believe in centralized authority.

The solution has to be about decentralization, to distribute power among many. Sounds familiar? Yes, it's a 2,500-year-old idea: democracy, Greek for "people" (dêmos) and "power" (krátos) – people power!

This is where the internet became the great opportunity. Centralization is dangerous, inefficient and will make a system vulnerable; if someone hacks it, we're toast. Decentralization, to link billions of nodes rather than to rely on one big database, is much, much safer. The concept of the internet is decentralization, much like a hydra (a minute freshwater aquatic invertebrate with a stalk-like tubular body). You can hack, close and kill any limb but the hydra never dies.

However, in the first two decades of the internet, the ones with power managed to get even more power with this new technology. Old business models were digitalized, so markets grew fast and profit margins increased as a result of lowered marginal costs. But with a new generation of entrepreneurs and start-ups, born in the internet-era, we are witnessing how old business models are becoming obsolete.

Google, Facebook and Amazon are, to be fair, not great examples of sharing power ... but they all created a business model based on the concept of decentralization. As individuals we search for answers, we reply and talk to each other about tips and tricks, we trade goods, and we create and consume entertainment. These internet companies are not content creators, they are just aggregating and analysing all the data we are feeding them, and with it they get to know us so they can serve us with constantly better, tailor-made solutions. They know what we want.

This pull-model – outside in – is the opposite of the old business models in which innovation, product development, distribution and marketing are pushed from the inside out. That's the opposite of knowing and serving each individual what they want.

You can hack,
close and kill
any limb but the
hydra never dies.

What is happening right now is that internet entrepreneurs have spotted an opportunity, since this change is happening in every industry. With the internet, the marketplace is global and totally open for new monopolies. Just take the concept of decentralization to any industry and go! Run as fast and far as you possibly can before anyone notices you and voilá, your head start might be enough to win the first phase, the monopoly phase.

Maybe you don't think of tech-entrepreneurs as monopolists, but that's what is being witnessed now. All these Silicon Valley start-ups that popped up in no time from nowhere managed to create a new monopoly. Or do you "Google" with different search engines, do you "Facebook" on many platforms?

CHAPTER TWELVE

THE **POWER**
OF
NETWORKS

*If you want to create
and capture lasting value,
look to build a monopoly.
Competition is for losers.*

– Peter Thiel

At first the IT (information technology) revolution was all about information and the ones who were in the business of providing information – the media – were challenged. Then having enough people online led to the birth of social media (interaction technology), and we started to use the information for trade and shopping. In this new e-commerce landscape, we started to talk about companies like Uber and Airbnb, which earned a reputation as creators of a new "sharing economy." Airbnb is a broker for short-term house rentals and Uber is a broker for transportation. Their business models have succeeded because they created new monopolies, the direct opposite of sharing. This phase will continue as long as the opportunity exists to outcompete old business models by launching new monopolies, thus there will be many Kodaks in the near future.

Then it's time for the next phase. The protocol era.

Sharing is nothing new; we always shared but with a small number of people. We shared with the ones we trusted. The only reason brokers are used is because we don't trust each other. So trust is the key to the long-term change and the foundation for a true peer-to-peer economy. As soon as we – as individuals – understand that we don't need a broker to manage trust, everything will change again. This problem was solved in 2008 with the introduction of Bitcoin, cryptocurrency or digital currency, and the Blockchain, a decentralized ledger, a network of trust.

Sharing economy.

We will get back to the topic of cryptocurrency in the No Money chapter. For now, let's just think about a world where trust isn't a problem. You and I can do business with no need for a bank in between, no need for big organizations, well-known brands or social networks with people we trust, because we don't need to trust people any more. We trust in technology, in protocol.

A global, borderless, decentralized network is based on billions of independent nodes that all carry the exact same constantly updated ledger. No one is in control and there is no database to hack or manipulate. Just like the internet, there is no one to call and order a system shutdown; no one can turn it off. The protocol phase will take us back to a relationship-based economy, where reputation is worth more than money. In the same way that any network model works. The ones who give are the ones who get. Win-win becomes a winning strategy rather than a cliché.

Of course, as always with new technology threatening old power, we will see early legislation in parts of the world to protect the old ways of doing business. But history taught us one thing about protectionism versus technology: the ones who are eager to legislate will just build walls and the future will keep on going outside those walls, not necessarily inside them.

The ones who are eager to legislate will just build walls and the future will keep on going outside those walls, not necessarily inside them.

Another interesting thing about decentralized trust networks is that we might be able to leave the system of representative democracy. In today's complex world, it hasn't been possible to involve every citizen in every decision, so we vote for professional politicians to represent us, which again gives power to just a few. But maybe that is about to change with full connectivity and decentralization.

With the crypto currency, this can be accomplished on a large scale. Etherium is one of the platforms that allows a network of peers to administer smart contracts without any central authority, so the technology is here.

If I believe you can make the best decision on a certain issue, I can delegate my vote to you, and everyone on the internet can see that I transferred it and you now have it. With this, a new form of liquid democracy is possible, to let any citizen at any time have their voice heard in the making of policy processes, even if they don't want to become full-time politicians. So every citizen has a vote for every issue on the table, and they can choose to delegate their vote to any person whom they believe is the best one to make an informed decision. Liquid democracy can be a combination of direct and indirect (representative) democracy. At first you might think this sounds crazy, to let everyone vote on every issue – what a mess!

But people said that about crowdsourcing knowledge (Wikipedia) or software (Linux) and tons of other examples. The source of the crowd has been far more relevant than anyone imagined and since there are still three billion people without access to the internet, we are at the beginning of the beginning. Crowdsourcing is the 21st century word for democracy.

Power to the people.

CHAPTER THIRTEEN

NO
BOSS

The empires of the future are the empires of the mind.

– **Winston Churchill**

Pancreatic cancer is a deadly disease, mainly because of late discovery. In most cases, the tumor grows in silence with no symptoms; on average, there is a ten-year period between cell mutation and the establishment of a primary tumor. Then it can take another ten years before the victim dies. Jack Andraka was only 15 years old when he witnessed how this cruel disease killed one of his close friends. He was told that early detection is crucial, but 85% of everyone diagnosed gets the news too late, primarily because of very expensive and inaccurate testing methods.

One day in school, Jack had a vision and instead of paying attention to his teacher he went online to search for answers – and found them! He discovered a possible solution on how to measure the level of mesothelin (a suspected cancer biomarker) with much greater accuracy and for a fraction of the previous cost. Jack explained his theory in an e-mail that was sent to 200 professors to get the needed support, and he got one positive reply from Anirban Maitra, professor of pathology and oncology at the John Hopkins School of Medicine. It turned out Jack's method is 168-times faster, 1/26th as expensive and 400-times more sensitive than old testing methods, and more than 90% accurate in detecting mesothelin, and it can also be used to detect other forms of cancer.

Pancreatic cancer is a deadly disease, mainly because of late discovery.

A teenager who educated himself on Google, Wikipedia and YouTube then managed to invent something to disrupt a world of scientists. This would not have been possible ten years ago.

History reminds us of the Isaac Newton quote: "If I have seen a little further it is by standing on the shoulders of giants." Of course, Jack Andraka deserves a standing ovation, but the great difference between Newton's time and Jack's is the internet. Anyone with an internet connection has access to more information than the world's most powerful man had just 20 years ago. This means that anyone can climb on anyone's shoulders to see as far and as long as they want to.

The answers were out there all the time; Jack found them and put the puzzle together.

Oppressed people are encouraged when they're aware of how many are in their ranks, march to the square to tell the dictator to step down. Anyone can find information and make reservations at holiday destinations without the need for brokers who used to dictate the marketplace. Satisfied and dissatisfied customers are posting reviews and telling others about their experiences of companies and their products with no need to pay any attention to the bagman who lost our attention. The gap between professionals and amateurs is tightening – crowdsourcing.

In the summer of 2008, Apple launched its Appstore, a marketplace for software for mobile devices. Until then, the telecommunications industry was all about hardware and only the biggest corporations were strong enough to compete by constantly launching new hardware. With the iPhone in 2007 and the new app-economy everything changed; now the market is a software market, open to developers from all over the world. All you need to compete is an idea and programming skills (something you can learn on the internet).

During the first five years of this new ecosystem, customers downloaded 50 billion applications and Apple paid its creators some $10 billion. Google does the same for Android with Google Play and at the time of writing this book the combined number of apps for sale in this new ecosystem is more than three million growing by more than 1,000 each day. One well-known success story is Angry Birds, a mobile game developed by three young Finnish students, Niklas Hed, Jarno Väkeväinen and Kim Dikert released in 2009. As of July 2015 the Angry Birds series of games have been downloaded more than three billion times collectively and the development company, Rovio Entertainment, is one of the world's leaders in mobile gaming.

This is a gold rush of our time and the three guys from Finland who started a few years ago with a mortgage on their parents' homes are as fascinating as any poor person who strikes it big.

Google Adwords is another example of how the internet is a power shift. As you know, there is advertising all over the internet, on pretty much any web page. There are ads when you search and there are ads (related to your queries) when you are browsing. This marketplace is just like the app-ecosystem, open to everyone who wants to find a buyer, and ad visibility is determined by auction. The salesperson will pick a target group and choose how much they are willing to spend, whereupon Google will tell hem how far that money will go. This means that anyone with a web page open to advertising can get revenue from displaying those ads, something completely exclusive to big media corporations just some years ago. Today thousands of people refer to themselves as "digital nomads" and as such make a living from many small rivers of online revenue, rather than a set income from an employer.

Trey Ratcliff is one of them. Trey was born blind in one eye and very interested in photography and technology. He studied computer science at the Southern Methodist University in Dallas and started to experiment on improving photographs with the use of new technology. In 2005, Trey started to blog about HDR, at the time a relatively unknown technology on how to combine multiple different exposures, with one motive: to give the end result a wider range of light and color. Five years later, Trey Ratcliff's blog, http://stuckincustoms.com, is the number-one travel photography blog in the world and, of course, very important for any marketer in the photo industry.

Today, Trey is traveling the world taking pictures. Every day he presents new striking images and stories to his world-wide audience and his business has evolved to books, films, workshops and lectures with a staff of ten full-time employees.

Companies that pollute, managers who try to hide the truth, bad products, and inhumane working conditions are going to be skeletons.

In Chris Anderson's book *The Long Tail*, published in 2004, the power shift from connectivity and information technology was explained with one sentence: "Why the future of business is selling less of more." Amazon is the obvious example. They were the first to make a fortune by selling fewer numbers of many books instead of the way booksellers used to do it, many sales of fewer books. According to Chris's theory, the tail is not just long, it is endless. So, the one who manages the logistics of offering everything that's out there will beat the old industries whose strategy is to offer one or at least a limited number of blockbusters to everyone. This is what's happening right now; we are leaving the industrial era and entering the era of tailor-made to everyone. The internet is the land of opportunity.

One equally important aspect of the power shift and the transparency that comes with it is that anyone can win. Companies that pollute, managers who try to hide the truth, bad products, and inhumane working conditions are going to be skeletons increasingly harder to hide now when the closet door is wide open and the light is on 24/7. Leaders in the corporate world and in politics are just starting to realize this; hence it is just the beginning. So far we have seen an increased interest in reputation, with new trends in public relations (PR) and corporate social responsibility (CSR).

Eventually leaders will understand the need for a holistic approach to value creation and the concept of a true win-win scenario for all stakeholders rather than a few shareholders. Putting money aside for social projects and PR-stunts that have little, if any, relevance for the core business isn't going to win any support. This is when the old form of capitalism with a simple purpose of making money will face its power shift. In the next era of capitalism, it will be much more difficult. The goal in any hierarchy has always been to reach the top, but in a network there is no top and the goal is to create a strong network. The ones who create value to many will be the winners, or more appropriately, the win-winners. This trend, for now just among a small number of leaders and companies, is referred to as conscious capitalism, where its followers – corporations and leaders – articulate societal goals instead of just monetary ones.

Just like with CSR, the understanding of what needs to be done will grow among leaders when these conscious capitalists start to show greater monetary results than competitors. And they will because of the power shift.

Jack Andraka has the power; Trey Ratcliff and the Finnish entrepreneurs have the power. You have the power. Everybody can win, and no one needs a boss to do it.

CHAPTER FOURTEEN

NO SCHOOL

When you judge another,
you do not define them,
you define yourself.

– Wayne Dyer

Knowledge is power. But what if everyone had access to the power? There has always been a tight correlation between education and wealth. The median income for a 40-year-old in the US without a high-school diploma in 2013 was $22,320; for those with a diploma $41,190; for those with a degree $76,293; and for those with an advanced degree $116,265.* Globally the difference is even more striking and the low quality of education in much of the developing world is no secret.

With the advances in technology and globalization, more pressure has been put on workers, who now constantly need to update their knowledge, so the importance of education will be even greater. Or maybe not.

It is so easy to fall for the old "go to school, study hard, get good grades and you will have a great future". But today you don't need a school, you just need an internet connection and the desire to learn. And you don't necessarily need to acquire any skills before you are able to use them. One of the greatest sources for education is YouTube tutorials. You want to learn to speak Spanish, play the guitar, troubleshoot the starter in a Yamaha outboard engine? Well it's all out there; it's all available on YouTube, just watch and follow. You want more? Project management? Data science? Music production? An MBA? There are thousands of massive open online courses (MOOCs) available, and with online universities like Coursera (www.coursera. org), millions of students from all over the world have access to many programs, some even for free.

The low quality of education in much of the developing world is no secret.

At the same time, the internet population will double this coming decade as tech companies like Google and Facebook are working on the "internet from the sky project" aimed at connecting everyone who still isn't online, with a grid of weather balloons, satellites and solar-powered airplanes. This means that every child in every rural village will have access to all the world's education and knowledge. Imagine the day that your chief information officer (CIO) suggests that a 14-year-old freelancer in Bharatpur offers the same work in one week for $42 as a 12-month, $1million project done the old fashioned way. This is phase one in the globalization of white-collar work. Not that every kid in Makambako will put on a white shirt, but they will definitely be able to compete with the ones who do, in Boston, Oslo, Singapore – everywhere.

Then comes phase two: smart machines.

What if we could build machines that not only do what the programmer tells them to do, but have the capacity to learn on their own and change in unpredictable ways, just like humans? Half a century of exponential growth in processing power means we are on the brink of a new era. The progress in areas like artificial intelligence (AI) and machine learning is very exciting and we already have many examples where machines can replace human brains. We are used to replacing humans with machines, like a tractor a crane or even a robot, but that has mainly been about replacing human muscles.

What if we could build machines that not only do what the programmer tells them to do, but have the capacity to learn on their own?

Today, we no longer build things like the pyramids using manpower; that's why most people in the developed world work in offices. Today, we are brain workers, not muscle workers.

But in the era of AI, computers and algorithms will replace brain workers.

When the IBM computer system Watson competed on *Jeopardy!* against former winners Brad Rutter and Ken Jennings in 2011, the world got the first glimpse of what is to come. The very best among us don't stand a chance.

Today, the Watson technology platform is used to solve serious problems like cyber-security and cancer. The internet is a jungle of data; it may be impossible for humans to collect, sort and analyse it, but it's not impossible for computers. When a computer learns how to understand the information, put it in context and detect connections, it can provide analysis and answers never imagined possible before. The "Watson for oncology" project is a great example of how smart machines can create value. By analysing the meaning and context of structured and unstructured data in clinical notes, Watson is assimilating individual treatment pathways with much greater accuracy than a human doctor could possibly do. Today the system is like a capable and knowledgeable colleague to doctors, but in the future it might very well replace much of the work they do. Think about it from a patient perspective: if you were able to choose between any human doctor and Watson with a documented 90% accuracy in treatment decisions. The same goes for lawyers, accountants, marketers … anyone working with collecting, sorting and analysing data to provide recommendations will face machine competition.

In May 2016, when Professor Ashok Goel told his students at Georgia Tech that his online teaching assistant for the entire semester, Jill Watson, was a computer, it made news around the world. The students had been communicating with a machine for five months and none of them had figured it out. Goel will do the same next year, but names will change and students will have to guess if they are dealing with a robot or not.

And what about exponential growth in the area of AI? If today's machine are smart like a small primitive brain, still not even aware of its existence, the next generation will have double that intelligence, and then double that. And onward it goes; there is no reason to believe technology will stop at the Einstein-level just because we humans didn't get any further.

What if AI proves to be not just 10% smarter than us but 10x or 100x? In a future like that, many of today's great problems such as climate change, cancer and poverty might turn out to be really primitive and simple problems, much like when we look back and think about the primitive problems and solutions of the Dark Ages.

Success in creating AI would be the biggest event in human history. Unfortunately, it might also be the last, unless we learn how to avoid the risks.

Or is this the beginning of the Dark Ages 2.0? Maybe even the Last Ages? Great thinkers like Stephen Hawking, Elon Musk, Bill Gates and Nick Bostrom are warning about the consequences of AI. "Success in creating AI would be the biggest event in human history. Unfortunately, it might also be the last, unless we learn how to avoid the risks," wrote Stephen Hawking in an op-ed published in *The Independent* in 2014.*

No matter what one thinks about today's advancements in technology, it is unlikely that the progress will stop, even if it is realized that this advancement might pose an existential risk. That notion didn't stop us from building and using the atomic bomb. This is why global collaboration instead of competition is the only possible way forward. Not only will conflict be the direct route to dystopia, since resources are limited, competition is most likely the wrong strategy if you want a better future.

In a future where billions of people have access to unlimited information and knowledge, and where computers are superior problem-solvers, it is very hard to believe that education will still be the key to wealth. As individuals, we will probably always enjoy the feeling of learning and mastering new skills; it's part of our self-actualization. But even though knowledge is valuable to us as individuals, it might not be valued from a societal perspective. Why would anyone pay for knowledge if it's abundant? The more you think about it, you will realize that the future of intelligence might very well be a no-brainer.

If we are stuck in competition and machines are taking our jobs, this of course is a threat. If the end of work equals the end of wealth to workers, it doesn't work. However, if we use the technology to solve our problems and serve our needs, and share the outcome, then we will all be free to do whatever we want with the time we have. The keyword in that sentence is *share*, and this is where the new generation comes in. The sharing economy is a new economic paradigm, where we share assets. It's not only a better, more efficient system, it is a crucial shift necessary to embrace the future of abundant knowledge and super intelligence.

* https://www.stlouisfed.org/household-financial-stability/the-demographics-of-wealth/essay-2-the-role-of-education

* http://www.independent.co.uk/news/science/stephen-hawking-transcendence-looks-at-the-implications-of-artificial-intelligence-but-are-we-taking-9313474.html

CHAPTER FIFTEEN

NO
MONEY

*The attitude of gratitude
is the highest yoga.*

– Yogi Bhajan

Do you remember the day, back in March 1989, when a computer scientist named Tim Berners-Lee proposed something he referred to as the World Wide Web?

Of course you don't! You and I were busy talking about things like the Exxon Valdez oil spill in Alaska and the movie *Rain Man*, which won the Academy Award for best picture that year. Worlds like TCP/IP, HTTP and WWW meant nothing to ordinary people like us.

Do you remember the day, back in 2008, when someone who called himself Satoshi Nakamoto proposed something referred to as Bitcoin? Again, of course not! We were all busy talking about Lehman brothers in 2008. (We still are.)

Almost a decade later, we are 100% focused on how to save the old system, instead of paying attention to what the concept of cryptocurrency and a decentralized ledger actually means. First, this is because the idea is complex and tricky to explain, which means it doesn't fit mainstream media, which wants everything in black or white. If you believe in newspapers, Bitcoin is bad: it's an extremely volatile currency backed by no solid value or any government, used by a few nerds who speculate and criminals who do money laundering. There have been headlines like "Bitcoin CEO Found Dead" even though the concept of a decentralized system means there is no such thing as a CEO.

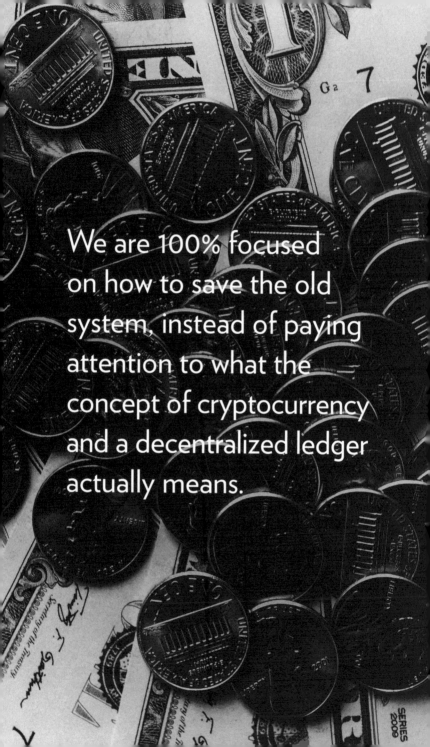

We are 100% focused on how to save the old system, instead of paying attention to what the concept of cryptocurrency and a decentralized ledger actually means.

Second, many think of Bitcoin as digital money, and therefor all discussions are focused on exchange rates to determine value. The currency is extremely volatile since it is an immature and small currency compared to any state (fiat) currency. But Bitcoin might be so much more than internet money; maybe we need to think of it as the internet of money. In that case, currency is just the first application, like e-mail was the first application of the internet.

If you think about cryptocurrency as the internet of money, maybe 2016 should be compared to 1998, eight years after Tim Berners-Lee introduced the World Wide Web. In 1998, there was no Google, Facebook or Amazon. No blogs, tweets or YouTube clips. Broadband and wifi were for few and we never imagined such a thing as a smartphone. To many of us, the value of internet was e-mail and not much more.

What does a decentralized autonomous trust network mean? What will be the killer app in the internet of money?

To most people, it's also hard to believe cryptocurrency could overthrow any state currency. But think about money. If you remember the movie *Dumb and Dumber*, you might recall the scene where Jim Carrey's character, Lloyd, emptied a suitcase full of money, but proudly announces that everything is noted on an IOU: "That is as good as money…those are I owe yous."
(https://www.YouTube.com/watch?v=7GSXbgfKFWg)

The comedy is actually a good analogy of our banking system. Any fiat currency is nothing but an "I owe you" (IOU) and the value depends only on trust. As long as the world trusts in the issuer, the system works, but if – for any reason – the trust weakens or disappears, that money is simply nothing but a piece of paper with some ink and bacteria.

Today many countries also replace physical money, coins and paper bills, with digital money. No need for anyone to write an "I owe you" on a piece of paper or carry suitcases full of money anymore; just check the mobile bank app and it will tell you the balance on your account (how much the bank owes you). Those are "I owe yous" … "they are as good as money". As long as you trust your bank this works, even though you know that no bank in the world can pay its debt.

When the financial crisis of 2008 occurred, we witnessed how vulnerable the world economy and the financial system are, and since there was no fundamental change at that time, unavoidably there is more to come. In this case, we don't necessarily need new innovative technology to disrupt the old; the system is probably bad enough to kill itself.

Just like with the internet, Bitcoin and Blockchain are built on the idea of decentralization, where transactions are verified by independent nodes that also carry a copy of the ledger.

Just like with the internet, Bitcoin and Blockchain are built on the idea of decentralization, where transactions are verified by independent nodes that also carry a copy of the ledger. Since there are millions of nodes, it is impossible to hack or tamper with the ledger; it would be like taking over all the web servers in the world simultaneously. Verification is done by cryptology. Computers compete to solve a question; this is what is called mining. This is also the foundation for inflation, since miners are incentivized with new Bitcoin. Unlike fiat currency, no one politician can do anything to influence the currency and inflation is predictable all the way until the end, where the total amount of Bitcoins will be 21 million somewhere around the year 2140 when the total supply of Bitcoins will cease to increase.

I am not saying Bitcoin will be relevant in 2140; no one knows. The point is that with this technology we don't need any middlemen to establish trust.

In the future, people will talk about today's centralized banking system as a slow, costly and extremely inefficient system, and we have already talked about all of the security issues. A database can be hacked and in banking this is a huge problem; just one more reason why we shouldn't have just one database.

In the case of Bitcoin, I don't believe we in the developed world will start the transformation. We have too much to lose. But most people on the planet don't. Three billion people in the world don't even have a bank account and almost five billion lack access to the international SWIFT transaction system. These people have everything to win with the internet of money. They will be able to trade from mobile phones, make micro-transactions, and cross borders at minimum fees without asking for permission. When the time comes for this revolution in global trade, the crash of 2008 will seem like a walk in the park. Bankers, as well as politicians, will probably argue for legislation to protect the ponzi schemes of the fiat era. To the rest of the world, they will sound just like Jim Carrey's character, Lloyd.

It's all "I owe yous", there is no money.

CHAPTER SIXTEEN

NO CAR

In less than 20 years, owning a car will be like owning a horse.

– Elon Musk

It's easy to go anywhere in the digital world, but if you want to leave home and travel somewhere in the physical world, it is a bit more complicated. Millions of people spend hours commuting every day, and congestion and air pollution are a growing problem in every megacity, often a direct threat to further growth and prosperity. But the trend is nowhere near slowing down; today almost four billion people live in cities and this number is expected to double by 2050.

The automobile used to be a symbol of freedom, but to urban millennials it is rather the opposite. Cars are used on average for one hour per day, which means they stay parked for 23 hours. To own a car is a very expensive and inefficient way to create the freedom of mobility. And since the fossil fuel industry and the automotive industry are focused on protecting old business models instead of innovation, the majority of cars are still propelled by gasoline. Luckily the car industry is being disrupted right now. It started some years ago with the concept of car-sharing in metropolitan areas, then tech-companies like Google invested in projects to develop self-driving cars and now Tesla, a company founded in 2003, is leading the transformation to sustainable transportation.

As I'm writing this, Tesla Motors just launched "Model 3", the first mass-market electric vehicle for less than $40,000 that will go 200 miles on a charge, and the numbers are just crazy! Pre-sales topped first-year projections in less than 24 hours; 115,000 people ordered the car and paid a $1,000 deposit before they actually knew what they were buying. The first week after the unveiling, Tesla received more than 325,000 orders, and consumers expect the product to be delivered within one year of their order. "That corresponds to about $14 billion in implied future sales," the company said*.

Tesla Model 3 is to fossil-fuelled cars what the Model T Ford was to horses.

But just like always, the dying patient still doesn't understand what's happening. In an interview with The Verge*, Ford CEO Mark Fields had this to say about Tesla: "Tesla has done a very nice job of raising awareness of electrified vehicles. They cater to a high-end consumer, where the Tesla is usually their second, third, or fourth vehicle. It's not their only vehicle. Our approach has been to give consumers the power choice, whether plug-in hybrids or overall electrified vehicles, and be true to our brand and accessible." This is to me the exact same words uttered by Nokia managers when Apple launched the first iPhone in 2007. When Apple introduced a user-friendly device for mobile internet, it was ignorant to think about the iPhone as a product and compare its features with other handsets. Suddenly there were hundreds of mobile phones in one corner and then there was the iPhone alone on the other end. People didn't wait in line for hours to just buy a new phone; they had been seduced by the dream of hassle-free access to the internet from their pockets.

Everyone, including the Ford CEO, should know that the ambition of Elon Musk, the founder of Tesla, is much greater than to "own the high-end of the market". He has very publicly said it from day one, ten years before the spectacular Model 3 launch: "As you know, the initial product of Tesla Motors is a high-performance electric sports car called the Tesla Roadster. However, some readers may not be aware of the fact that our long-term plan is to build a wide range of models, including affordably priced family cars. This is because the over-arching purpose of Tesla Motors (and the reason I am funding the company) is to help expedite the move from a mine-and-burn hydrocarbon economy toward a solar electric economy, which I believe to be the primary, but not exclusive, sustainable solution."

If you haven't seen it, the unveiling event is a fantastic showcase of visionary and inspirational leadership. Put this book aside and search YouTube for "Tesla Model 3 unveiling". Now watch how Elon Musk uses the first five minutes to talk about the why, before he goes on to show the product. "It's very important to accelerate the transition to sustainable transport. We have record-high CO_2 levels. This is really important for the future of the world." Tesla is not only a product; people are bringing sleeping bags and tents to hear him speak, because they want to buy the dream about a better future.

Millions of people spend hours commuting every day, and congestion and air pollution are a growing problem in every megacity, often a direct threat to further growth and prosperity.

As a Tesla driver myself, I would have a hard time going back to any fossil-fuel car. Sometimes it actually feels like I am witnessing the shift we are in live; like the day I stopped at a Supercharger and this poor guy next to me tried to cool down his over-heated old Volvo. The car was making noise and smoke came from under the hood; it felt like I was witnessing a snorting horse carriage from the quiet future. And of course it doesn't stop with fossil-free, clean cars, I just got auto-steering in a software update so now I don't have to do all the driving myself any more. Between the launch in November 2015 to May 2016, Tesla logged 47 million miles of driving. Data from cars all over the world is being used to further develop these systems by machine learning. Many tech companies and auto companies are focusing on the concept of self-driving cars and the main problem is no longer about technology but rather about law. Who is going to be held responsible if there are no drivers? That's a big question; 17 out of 17 accidents with autonomous Google cars are caused by other motorists who have a really hard time driving with a 100% correct driver on the streets.It is tricky to mix humans and machines, but we will get there: 94% of all accidents are caused by humans, so we have to get there. And when traditional automakers like Volvo are introducing concept cars where the driver can choose between three different modes – drive, create or relax – it tells us the driving era is over. "Driving" in the future will be a time to watch movies, play games, and meditate or rest.

It might be optimistic to believe that this will happen within a decade or two, but it is happening faster than we think. And when it does, we don't have to consume cars as products anymore. In the future, we can share self-driving cars and we won't need to own cars but we can digitalize it as a service and thereby start to consume cars in a transportation cloud.

You don't need to own a car; you need transportation.

* https://www.teslamotors.com/blog/the-week-electric-vehicles-went-mainstream?utm_campaign=Blog_Model3_040716&utm_source=Twitter&utm_medium=social

* http://www.theverge.com/2016/4/7/11333288/ford-ceo-mark-fields-interview-electric-self-driving-car-software

* https://www.teslamotors.com/blog/secret-tesla-motors-master-plan-just-between-you-and-me

CHAPTER SEVENTEEN

NO
OIL

There is a reason it is called fossil fuel – it is an outdated method of getting power.

– **Alexandra Paul**

Five out of the ten largest corporations in the world today are oil companies. Sinopec Group, Royal Dutch Shell, China Natural Petroleum, Exxon Mobile and BP have combined revenues of more than $2 trillion and almost three million employees. These businesses affect everyone and everything on Earth. This is what makes the world go round, this is your retirement fund.

Our strategy should be to kill it all.

Oil, coal and gas served us well through industrialization and worked well when there was only one or two billion people on earth. But today we are seven billion and we have already burned way too much fossil fuels. The long-term warming trend looks like a stock-broker's dream chart, constantly climbing and breaking new record levels, despite the cries of scientists and experts from all over the world for a long time. Global warming is driving the world's climate into uncharted territory. We will probably not be able to stop global warming at the critical 2° Celsius increase, which is the target that has been set to prevent dangerous uncontrolled interference with our climate system. We don't need to wait to see disastrous consequences like rising sea levels and extreme weather causing death and unmeasured damage. To quote Elon Musk: "We are running the most dangerous experiment in history right now, which is to see how much carbon dioxide the atmosphere can handle before there is an environmental catastrophe." There are still climate deniers out there,

Oil, coal and gas served us well through industrialization and worked well when there was only one or two billion people on earth.

but they remind us of the Earth-is-round-deniers of the 15th century, although we should be way past that level of ignorance now. One more almost-forgotten detail is the fact that we are running out of fossil fuels. We are withdrawing what took the Sun millions of years to create without making any deposits, so there will be none left for future generations. No matter how hard the consequences are, the extreme position is to advocate for no change.

At the same time, solar energy is in a steady exponential trend, doubling its market share every two years. Solar currently supplies 2% of global electricity up from 0.5% in 2012. In two years that will be 4%, in four years 8%, and in six years 16%. Analysts predict the linear pattern, a 10% solar market share in 20 years, but if we continue with the exponential trend, we will pass 100% in only 12 years. Of course, 100% is unlikely, and energy is not only about technology as in what we can produce, but more so about politics, what we want to achieve. Nevertheless, I didn't write this book for cynics.

Today, five of the ten largest corporations in the world are oil companies. We have to kill their businesses and we can.

We are running the most dangerous experiment in history right now, which is to see how much carbon dioxide the atmosphere can handle before there is an environmental catastrophe.

Future leaders are already doing it. Piyush Goyal, energy minister of India, says the country is on track to lead the world as champion for underdeveloped, clean tech and clean energy. "I sincerely believe that what the West is doing in this respect is anti-development and ignores the fight against climate change." He said this in April 2016*, at the release of a 15-point action plan where the giant country presented ambitious goals of how to lead the transformation to renewable energy.

You don't need to focus on carbon dioxide or price volatility to understand why investing in coal and oil is a risky strategy.

Renewables will kill fossil fuels simply because it is technology, not fuel, and as such it will get more efficient and cheaper with time. Simple as that!

Add to that the change facing all other industries that will have an impact on demand, like international shipping. What if 3D-printing means we can ship information instead of stuff?

And then you have the risk of policy, a retroactive carbon tax should sound scary enough to keep investors away from oil.

So forget about 'peak oil' we're at peak thirst.

* https://youtu.be/uURYQSsAN_8

CHAPTER EIGHTEEN

NO
JOB

*True happiness is when
the love that is within
us finds expression
in external activities.*

– Mata Amritanandamayi

What if we could build machines that did not only do what their programmers taught them to do, but machines that learned and changed with experience and from other machines? The topic of AI and machine learning is nothing new – in theory. But it's really happening now, as cheap processing power and connectivity lay the foundation for a perfect storm. We already know computers can beat humans at playing games like chess and *Jeopardy*! As always, when comparing the potential of computers to human intellect, it is impossible until it's not. Today we must ask ourselves if there is anything in the future that a machine will not be able to do better than a human being.

We don't need to look in the science-fiction section to read about human brains being replaced by machines. In the financial industry, many traders and analysts have already lost their jobs to algorithms juggling more data than any human being could crunch in a lifetime. In healthcare, the IBM Watson computer is collaborating with oncologists to make better treatment decisions in the fight against cancer. The combination of a vast quantity of data, tutoring from specialists every time they feed the computer results and the ability to remember and analyse without bias when making treatment decisions makes Watson the best doctor in the world.

Next up will be lawyers, accountants, project leaders and marketers. Automation used to be associated with muscle power and blue-collar workers, but now we are about to automate the brain power of anyone in white collars.

To argue for the correlation between technology and increased unemployment rates is to be a Luddite, and the story of how workers destroyed machines in the 19th century is told to prove how wrong they were. "Life is so much better today." But is that the whole truth, and will technology always bring increased wealth? In today's society, we distribute wealth by work, therefore it is important to have a job even to people who don't create value; they might even work with something that is a problem.

The energy industry is one example. In Germany, the transformation toward green energy is growing at record speed, with the most ambitious strategy among industrialized countries. Having said this, at the same time thousands of workers are doing everything they can to protect their jobs in the brown coal-mining industry. This is despite the fact that these power plants are among the largest sources of CO_2 emissions in the world. These workers are creating toxic gas. No one would argue to protect a job like that if we didn't value work.

Millions of people work with something that might be positive for the GDP but nothing else. This problem should be added to the fact that the world's population is growing toward ten billion people and the average age of the population is getting older and older. And we are in the beginning of the robotics era, in which we can expect increased automation.

To say that everyone might not be needed might not be an extreme position.

Jobless growth is a new, disruptive trend. So far, economic growth was always associated with decreased unemployment rates, but that might not be the case any longer. And no matter what you think or believe, there is no one who knows for sure. Perhaps we need to talk about a scenario where we don't need everyone to work.

How will that work?

When the polling institute Gallup asked workers from 142 nations around the world about work engagement, one more problem became obvious: only 13% are engaged in the work they do. That means 87% spend at least eight hours every workday doing something they would rather not. How does that sound from a human-resources perspective?

In Germany, the transformation toward green energy is growing at record speed.

Try to do this exercise without any bias. Think about work as a way to solve problems and create value, and then try to think about why we should work if we could solve those problems and create value without doing it. What if machines solved our problems? Would we still have to work and why?

This is not to say that people don't want to work. It is merely to say that maybe people in a totally free society can work with whatever vision, dream or task they like instead of working for someone else. We know that with the current system, 87% of the population are not engaged and people are fighting to protect jobs that are killing our environment. We might look back one day and talk about this just the way we talk about slavery some centuries ago. People are not free to do what they want with their lives, and with technology we might be able to fix that problem. In theory this is simple. We only need abundance instead of scarcity. If machines can provide us with abundance in food, water, energy and healthcare, then it will no longer be a necessity to work. In such a scenario, it will obviously only be a question of distribution and sharing. And maybe it is not a question of wait and see, but rather like the chicken and egg problem – which comes first?

Should we free workers to see if that has a positive impact on attitudes toward new technologies like green energy? What would happen to the German brown-coal workers if we paid them to stop spewing poison into the atmosphere?

If you think that we can't afford it, think again. Or call Mario "we will do whatever it takes" Draghi: he will tell you we can print as much money as needed to save the banking system. Can't we do the same to save the environment? The fact is that no one knows if giving money to people would be positive or negative for a state's finances and there are currently many initiatives being considered and experiments looking into the so-called Unconditional Basic Income. Most Western countries already do provide a state income in some way. We pay for children to grow and study until they are of working age; we then pay people as they get older, after the age of 65 for their pensions. So we are already doing it. The combination of a free market economy and a generous welfare system has proved to be a very strong model for a safe and healthy society. With the Unconditional Basic Income, we don't need much administration either.

If this sounds challenging – breathe. Or for more information on this topic of Basic Income, read economist Guy Standing's book *The Precariat*. Then read Jeremy Rifkin's book *The Zero Marginal Cost Society*, to understand how the emerging internet of things is taking us to an era of nearly free goods and services.

Maybe time will be free in the future. We will be able to do whatever we want, and even though that might sound like a dream, it will probably be quite challenging.

What do you want to do with your time?

CHAPTER NINETEEN

NO
COUNTRY

When one tugs at a single thing in nature, he finds it attached to the rest of the world.

– John Muir

The British people just voted to leave the European Union. The "Brexit" might look very negative when we think about the next quarter, but it is not necessarily so if we try the next quarter-century perspective. Nationalism, borders and walls are on the rise among voters but that doesn't change the fact that we already live in a borderless network society where just about anything can be done in cyberspace with a mobile phone. As long as the Brits don't do a www.exit and leave the internet, they still live in the network society and there is no nation that can withstand the power of networks.

The US is the most obvious example; they have spent trillions of dollars and thousands of lives fighting the war on terrorism since the 11 September 2001 attacks, and the outcome is that terrorist organizations are stronger and more globalized than ever before.

Problems like extreme ideologies or global competition among workers don't care about borders. Nor do opportunities. We will most likely continue with the concept of nations for a long time, but that doesn't mean nations are relevant from the old perspectives of power. In the network society, nations and flags might become symbols like kings and queens, rather than institutions of power. In this time of transition, the gap between the ones who understand the power of networks and the ones who lose old positions will continue to widen. This is the foundation for populist politicians, who will have a hard time when they get elected.

Trillions of dollars and thousands of lives fighting the war on terrorism.

Software and networks will disrupt nations, as well as most traditional industries in the next ten years and with that most of today's jobs will disappear. This is creating social problems and stress, but it is actually great news for the future. We need disruptive change to battle serious problems and the power of networks is eventually what will unite human beings and even help us prevent threats, such as terrorism. The best way to defeat an evil ideology is to demonstrate the better lives people lead with other beliefs. Throughout history the pen was often mightier than the sword, and with a global borderless information network we have the power of billions of pens. No country on Earth can compete with that.

CHAPTER TWENTY

ASK WHY

It is not that we have a short time to live, but that we waste a lot of it.

– Lucius Seneca

"What will happen to people if machines take all the jobs?" I am often asked this question, and my reply is always the same: Why do you work?

The "what we do" is the easy question to answer: an occupation, expertise, title or company. We are used to talking about what we do all the time, but "why" we do it is a tough question, and the most common answer is "because I have to". This is not so inspiring, but unfortunately it is the common answer. As mentioned before, 87% of employees are sleepwalking through their workdays, putting time – but not energy or passion – into their work. Human beings are working because they have to. But there is no reason to believe that this isn't going to change. Just think about how much work has changed throughout the years. If we could travel back to the 18th century and tell a farmer that in the future we'll create so much food that we'll have more than we need, that we will throw away almost half of it, and we'll have very few farmers (do you know one?), that farmer would feel doubtful.

Many economists refer to this kind of thinking when they talk about the future challenges in the labour market. "Don't be a Luddite; we will create new jobs." But economists often rely on history and extrapolate data, and in this case they might forget about the new growing trend called "jobless growth". So far, the number of new jobs created in the past decade doesn't come close to the numbers of jobs that have been lost to automation

– and the speed of this decline is increasing. Many experts have studied this by comparing what we do today with what we can expect to automate in the coming 10 to 20 years. They have all come to the same conclusion: that the developed world will have lost almost half of today's jobs by 2030. This means half of the work force will have to come up with new jobs in 20 years. I'm not saying this is impossible, I'm just saying it sounds like a bold – and stupid – bet. What if we fail? What if we do nothing and believe that somehow, someone will come up with new jobs, and unemployment rates will be in double digits everywhere in 10 to 20 years?

I believe a good yoga workout is better. Let's stretch our minds by trying to free ourselves from everything we "know" from the past. Let's try to reason first from principles, rather than by analogy.

If it makes it easier to get the practice going, imagine that we are just a few people stranded on an uninhabited island. What do we need to do? We obviously have some problems that we need to solve, like finding water, food, shelter, health care and so on. Now, let's pretend a machine, like a smart robot, came with us to the island. This machine is capable of solving all our problems so that we don't have to work. This means that we will be free to do whatever we want with our time. Does that really sound so bad?

I can hear you thinking, "But I'm not on a desert island with a magical robot; I need money." Actually this is not really true, either. Let's go back to reason from the first principle. Wherever we may be, we will need water, food and shelter. These are represented on Maslow's hierarchy of needs, whereas money is actually nowhere to be found on the hierarchy. Work and money are means, rather than needs. That's the system we have created, but if someone would take care of our needs – like when we were babies – we would not need to work or have money.

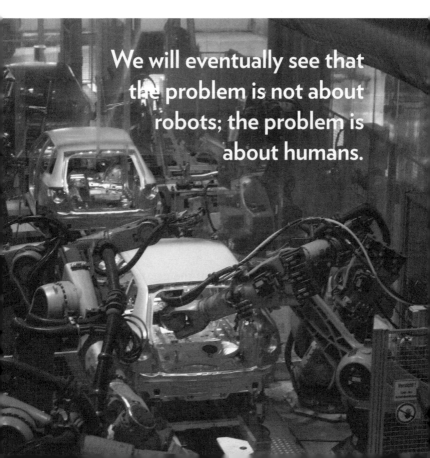

We will eventually see that the problem is not about robots; the problem is about humans.

When we think about increased automation and technology replacing human workers, we will eventually see that the problem is not about robots; the problem is about humans. If technology eventually gives us everything we need, we just have one problem – to share the outcome. And this is probably a serious problem because so far humans have not been very good at sharing.

Sharing is a question about economy – how to spend resources – and the most successful system (so far) has been the capitalistic free market economy. To make this thinking exercise easier, we will not challenge that system. Let's assume that technology is taking care of all our needs and we share the outcome in a free market. We will need money to buy products and services from all the machines, so the owners of the robots also need us to have money. If one guy owns all the technology and the rest of us are unemployed without money, the game would be over, just like when someone wins in the game Monopoly. A market economy doesn't work if the market doesn't have any purchasing power. It means the game is over, so the true problem is about redistribution of wealth rather than automation.

Inequality is probably one of the greatest challenges of our time. And it's no longer just about rich and poor countries. First of all, globalization has reduced the wealth gap on a global level as jobs – and wealth – have moved from workers in the US and Europe to people in Asia. But this has been at the cost of growing gaps on local levels. Second, the concentration of wealth is growing faster than the economy as a whole, as shown by economist Thomas Piketty.

One example of how the wealth distribution problem could be solved in a future with machine workers is the Unconditional Basic Income, where every citizen will get enough money to cover basic needs without any demand for counter-performance. This idea is currently being examined in Canada, Finland and the Netherlands. Opponents of this idea claim that it will be too expensive and lead to stagnation because no one would be incentivized to do anything. On the other hand, supporters believe that there is nothing more expensive to society than poverty, that the provision of a basic income could be like venture capital for poor people and result in a boom of entrepreneurship with people who work to fulfill their own dreams rather than the ones of a boss.

I believe one mistake we make when we think about the future of work is the assumption that we will quit working if don't have to work, that people are lazy and lack dreams.

We will work, but maybe we will stop talking about "what" we do and start talking about "why" we do it.

CHAPTER TWENTY-ONE

SUPPORT OTHERS

Good leadership has always been the exception, not the norm.

– Tomas Chamorro-Premuzic

We've heard about ping-pong tables at the office, free food, childcare and laundry for employees but what about paid paid vacation that was introduced earlier in this book? Paid paid, as in salary plus the cost of the vacation trip for your family, that is.

This concept was introduced by Bart Lorang, CEO of tech firm FullContact in 2012. Lorang was on holiday with his wife in Egypt and realized he was doing everything but enjoying the pyramids. Constantly connected to the office, texting and e-mailing made him think about the importance of disconnecting and about what he as a leader could do to make this happen. "We'll be a better company if employees disconnect," Lorang told the board back home, so they decided to incentivize them.

From that day, FullContact decided to give any employee $7,500 extra to pay for taking a vacation. But there is a catch: he or she *must* be off the grid – no e-mails, no calling work, absolutely no work whatsoever. Of course nobody complained; they've even started a company photo album for all the vacation pictures and Lorang says the move turned out to be of great value. It's easier to attract and keep talented people and even more important, the crew have more energy to be innovative and creative because they have time to disconnect more often.

Smartphones are just like a bowl candy for our brains, and just like with any addiction the brain will reward us for behaviour that might be bad for us. Studies say we check our phone on average 150 times per day on average. At the same time, studies say we need (at least) 20 minutes without distraction before we are really able to focus on any task...

And next comes virtual reality (VR): "Hey, check this out! I'm on stage with Beyonce in Paris, wanna try it out?" VR is candy intravenous. Now, to any junkie the idea of never being sober might sound great, but this is not a sustainable strategy. Without responsible digital behaviour and maybe every now and then a total detox, we will be lost, constantly distracted.

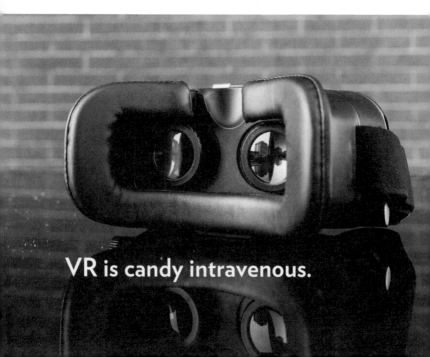

VR is candy intravenous.

This means there are three realities in today's life. First there is the reality of nature and everything surrounding us. Then there is the reality inside of us, everything that goes on in our minds. And now there is a virtual reality, as well. We communicate with people, order pizza and chase Pokemon's with connected devices that are becoming as real as the old two realities of nature and mind. To cope with this stress, we will have to disconnect not only from the distraction of our thoughts, but also from the constant noise of the virtual reality. But this is challenging to many leaders, who think of information technology as a means to increase productivity, and who still haven't understood the value of – and the basic human need to – come closer to nature and awareness in the present moment.

What would a manager like Henry Ford have said about the need for employees to disconnect and to pay for their vacation? Ford once uttered the words, "Why is it every time I ask for a pair of hands, they come with a brain attached?"

Managing used to be about control. This comes from the industrial era, where workers were suppliers of muscle power, a pair of hands, to do what they were told, not asked to improvise or innovate, question or change anything. Work was hard but rarely complex, so it was easy to replace anyone who didn't play by the rules or was not willing to please the manager.

In the globalized information age, we have outsourced muscle work and all become brain workers. We've left factories for office buildings and switched from blue collars to white.

The 21st-century version of the Henry Ford quote would be: "Why is it that every time I ask for a brain they leave it back home and come with only a pair of hands?" In this version, workers are supposed to bring knowledge, creativity and the ability to engage with others. If managers want their organizations to be agile, it's unrealistic to expect them to know and understand everything their employees are there to do. Innovation has to come from underneath, not delegated from top down.

To get this out from the team and encourage innovation, managers need to transform themselves from controllers to supporters. The most important task for any manager today is to understand what they can do to help their employees. Thereby managers, just like parents or teachers, need to do their best to become superfluous.

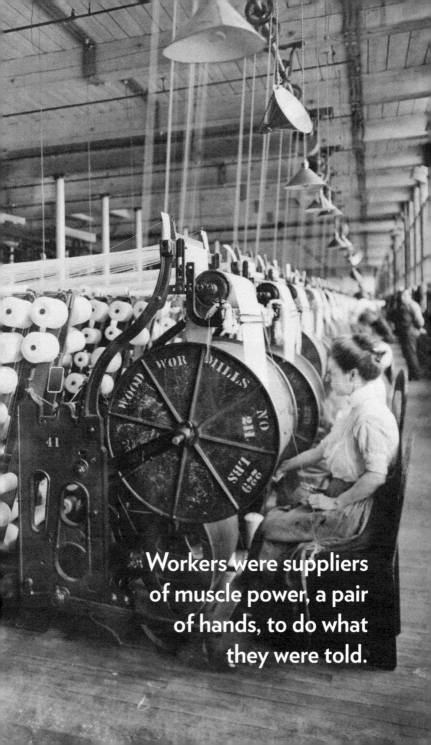

Workers were suppliers of muscle power, a pair of hands, to do what they were told.

CHAPTER TWENTY-TWO

THE PURPOSE OF LIFE IS TO LIVE A PURPOSEFUL LIFE

In the end, only three things matter: How much you loved, how gently you lived and how gracefully you let go of things not meant for you.

– Gautama Buddha

A couple of years ago, I witnessed a team of Tibetan monks create art on a table by pouring colored sand in different shapes and fine patterns all over the big square space. This is called a sand mandala. They were working on it for three full days during a conference I attended in San Francisco. Then at the end of the last day, when the work was completed for everyone to see, a spectacular piece of art rich in small details, they cleaned it up, just like that. All the beautiful patterns, all the colors, mixed together in a trashcan now full of greyish sand. Three days of work disappeared in a minute. The point, of course, was to symbolize the Buddhist belief in the transitory nature of material life. The joy must be in the work itself rather that the outcome.

I believe this is a great way to think about the future as well. It is not a destination, so we will never get there. We are alive for a very short time, which means we are conscious to experience this moment. All the joy and happiness is here, right now, in this present moment. This is it and no matter what we make out of it we will all end just like the grey sand.

Dust to dust.

Sand mandala.

This moment even used to be the future we were thinking about, until now. If we always think about getting somewhere else, accomplish something more, we will miss the beauty and the joy. Life is never not *now*. And whatever work you do, it will eventually be wiped away just like the sand mandala.

The purpose of life is to live a purposeful life. And leaders who offer purpose are the leaders we will follow.

CHAPTER TWENTY-THREE

BE A
POSSIBILIST

You cannot always control what goes on outside. But you can always control what goes on inside.

– Wayne Dyer

Are you an optimist or a pessimist? I get this question quite often in all parts of the world when I talk about the future. By reading this far, you know the answer is neither. The future will not be good or bad, it will be both, just like today. We have to be possibilists! Just like today, tomorrow will provide problems and it will be possible to solve many of them. We might fear problems, but they are not only bad. We want to solve them, not only because we have to (we enjoy solving small problems like crossword puzzles), but because the work itself will create a feeling of meaning and purpose, and that is really important.

Our solutions will become more and more disruptive by nature, as explained throughout this book, and this is essentially something good: we need disruptive change to solve many of todays huge problems, since many old solutions are way too slow. But disruption also means more stress, not only to organizations, but to us as individuals. The fact that so many people are stressed about the future might be one of our greatest challenges.

The future used to be something very exiting when we talked about it; science fiction was popular in my childhood. But over the last two decades the future has switched to become something many people fear. There are studies to prove that a majority of people actually think many problems and trends are much worse and more negative than they actually are. Swedish professor Hans Rosling and his team at the Gapminder Foundation does a good job trying to describe the world by facts, an contrast to the mainstream media narrative, but populist politicians in all democracies are working hard to convince voters that everything is going in the wrong direction.

While we should be more focused on following our dreams and purpose, we are set to self-destruct because of fear. We waste time to get more of something we already have and to fix problems already fixed. So we work even harder to become more and more vulnerable.

Lets just assume we will die tomorrow. Time's up! What would change? Many things, I guess.

And how do we dare treat time as an abundant resource just because we don't know when it will end? If you have to choose between having a great moment right now or a great moment in the future, you might as well pick the now. If you think about it, you have to choose the great now, since you know for sure that you are alive to experience it. To wish for something in the future is way riskier than the now, simply because you might be dead.

And no matter how hard life is, there is always something to be grateful for; even the most miserable human being alive is at least alive and thereby free to decide what they think. Holocaust survivor Viktor Frankl came up with a concept called logotherapy, a form of existential analysis, founded on the belief that it is the striving to find meaning in one's life that is the primary, most powerful motivating and driving force in humans. This notion helped him to survive the Nazi death camp, where everything but the freedom to think was taken away from him.

CHAPTER TWENTY-FOUR

GOOD LUCK!

*It is often said that before
you die your life passes before
your eyes. It is in fact true.
It's called living.*

– Terry Pratchett

As humans, we are gradually changing the way we think about the world. What is normal today was unbelievable 100 years ago, and people alive then would freak out if we could get them here instantly. The same goes for us. We think it is perfectly normal to have a hearing device, but scary to talk about cyborgs. I believe the singularity will come and it will then be impossible to define a human being. We will probably be able to download our mind and thereby be able to share and move memories and experiences between hosts (bodies).

Of course this sounds creepy today, but doesn't it also sound interesting? Maybe you and I live in a time where it will be possible to change bodies when our old ones are useless or hurting too much. Maybe we live in a time where artificial intelligence and robots will help us create an abundance of everything essential: clean energy, drinking water and healthy food, without any need for humans in hard labour. Maybe we will understand that the only problem, and the only sustainable strategy, is sharing, and this can become the foundation of a new economic paradigm. These are not predictions; the future is not to be predicted, it is to be created. These are possibilities and we will explore them since we are possibilists.

To tie this up, I will try to summarise and again explain why you want to explore ancient philosophy and the yogi mindset.

We are alive in the exponential age. This means that the speed of change will continue to increase, and as a consequence we will experience more change and with that comes more uncertainty. Therefore, learning how to live with uncertainty and insecurity is the only security. This is true for individuals as well as organizations. It is key to success for leaders.

And the solution is awareness. You need to disconnect to reconnect and learn to witness and challenge your thoughts. Don't believe in them, they are lying to you. "She made me sad, he makes me nervous, traffic is terrible." She never makes you sad, you do. He doesn't make you nervous, you do. You are the traffic! Awareness!

It is important to practise awareness in this way. To learn how to handle your inner life, just the way you handle life outside you. As human beings, we are aware of our existence, and we always believed in concepts such as religions, countries and money. Ideas like these can become very powerful if enough people believe in them, but they are still nothing but ideas. If you want to challenge your thoughts on this subject, the book *Sapiens* by Yuval Noah Harari is a fantastic read.

But powerful ideas and concepts are not only something going on in the outside world; we are full of ideas inside as well.

Everything in the universe is in constant motion and everything is interconnected.

One of the strongest ideas is the idea of a self. "I think, therefore I am." But even that is a creation of thoughts, not necessarily true. The concept of "you" is something that only exists in our minds. Everything in the universe is in constant motion and everything is interconnected. You are conscious and right now you are having a human experience, your conscious is inside a human body. When you sleep, you experience a different world. Dreams can be really weird compared to being awake.

The human brain is operating in one of five frequencies: alpha, beta, delta, gamma or theta. Beta is normal waking consciousness, where the majority of adults operate all day long. Theta is much slower and less distracted; adults go to this frequency with meditation and light sleep. Children up until five or six years of age often are in theta mode. This is why it sometimes seems that children don't pay attention or listen to what's "important" You are right, they are probably not paying attention, simply because they are absorbed in something else and totally present and dedicated to that experience. In theta, you experience visualizations, inspiration, creativity and great insights without disturbance from the constant alertness and inner voice of beta. When we say: "Behold the child inside you," this is the important takeaway.

You have to love yourself. But what is "you" if your body changes constantly? (You didn't mourn the last time you had a haircut and part of you was wiped away on the floor with a broom.) When you think about your existence, you realize that you are the creation of your own thoughts, that you are possessed about yourself. You think about you all the time. Every human being is like this; why do you think selfie-sticks are so popular?

So if you have low self-esteem, if you are mean to yourself, you will create a bad you. A suffering you.

Your body will die and no one knows what will happen to your conscious after death. The obvious risk you take is not loving this experience of this version of life while you had a chance.

Being alive is taking risks and the illusion of self is one of the really deep aha-moments. It might very well take you a lifetime of mindfulness to get there. But then again, the joy will be in the work itself, not the outcome.

I wish you the best of luck, we all depend on you!

FINAL THOUGHT FROM
STEFAN HYTTFORS

hyttfors   ...

hyttfors Residing in your true nature is better than understanding or practice. #YogaForLeaders

If you want to be part of this necessary trend of growing consciousness please be my co-writer! Share your stories, leadership ideas and mind stretching yoga exercises on facebook.com/yogaforleadersbook or Twitter and Instagram with hashtag #YogaForLeaders Namaste.